OCEAN

NORTH AMERICA

- Tropic of Cancer

HAWAIIAN ISLANDS

- Equator

• LINE ISLANDS

P O L Y N E S I A

IX
S

TOKELAU
ISLANDS

SAMOA
ISLANDS

COOK
ISLANDS

MARQUESAS
ISLANDS

SOCIETY ISLANDS

TAHITI

FRENCH
POLYNESIA

NIUE

- Tropic of Capricorn

OCEAN

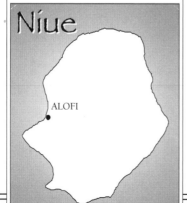

Níue

ALOFI

N

W   E

S

0   200   400   600   800
NAUTICAL MILES
MAP BY THOMAS CHILD

Niue
of Polynesia

Savage Island's
First Latter-day Saint Missionaries

Best Wishes

[signature]

8/12/04

Níue

of Polynesia

Savage Island's
First Latter-day Saint Missionaries

Robert Maurice Goodman

This work is dedicated
to those faithful and courageous
Niuean Saints who placed on the altar of life
all they had in order that the message
of the Restoration might come forth.

www.brookstonepublications.com

Printed in China

Edited by Marvin K. Gardner
Cover Design by Tom Child, Mazyne Inc.
Layout by Kari A. Todd

Library of Congress Control Number: 2002095634
ISBN 0-9664474-8-4

Contents

About the Author

ROBERT MAURICE GOODMAN, SR.,
was born on 4 May 1929 in Quantico, Virginia. As a young man he
served three years in the United States Air Force and then served nearly
three more years as a missionary for The Church of Jesus Christ of Latter-
day Saints in New Zealand and Niue.

He attended Virginia Commonwealth University (1957–59) and
Brigham Young University (1954–56). A real estate developer, broker, and
syndicator for many years, he is the author of *The Income Stream: A
Simplified Guide to Real Estate Investment Analysis*. He is currently president
of a real estate sales, rentals, and management company in Texas.

Active in community work, Robert Goodman served two terms as city
commissioner in Harlington, Texas, as president of the local Chamber of
Commerce in South Padre Island (1988–90), and as an instructor with
the National Association of Realtors.

A lifelong member of The Church of Jesus Christ of Latter-day Saints,
he has served as stake president, stake president's counselor, bishop,
bishop's counselor, and stake Young Men President. He is currently serving as president of the newly formed Powhatan Branch in Richmond,
Virginia.

He and his wife, the former Shirley Bernice Motschman, reside in
Powhatan, Virginia. They have seven children—Thomas, Robert Jr.,
Constance, Scott, Pamela, Lisa, and Kelly—and 18 grandchildren.

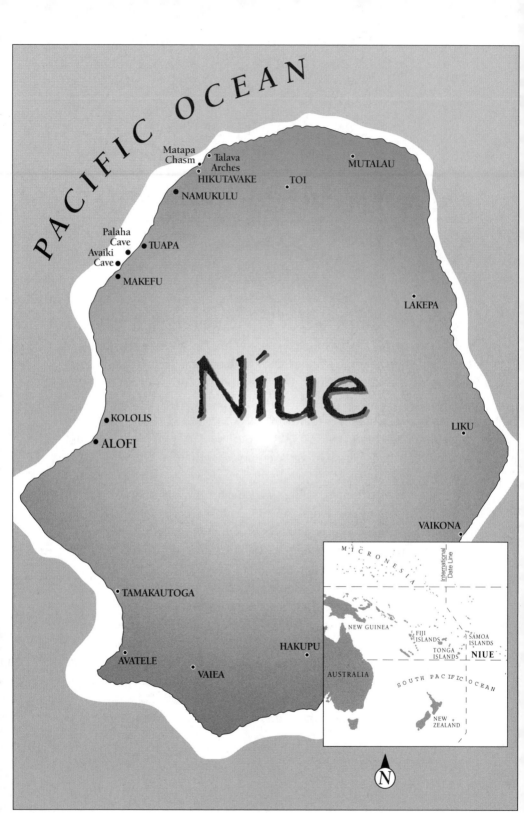

PACIFIC OCEAN

Matapa Chasm
Talava Arches
HIKUTAVAKE
NAMUKULU
MUTALAU
TOI

Palaha Cave
Avaiki Cave
TUAPA
MAKEFU

LAKEPA

Níue

KOLOLIS
ALOFI

LIKU

VAIKONA

TAMAKAUTOGA

HAKUPU

AVATELE
VAIEA

MICRONESIA
International Date Line
NEW GUINEA
FIJI ISLANDS
SAMOA ISLANDS
TONGA ISLANDS
NIUE
AUSTRALIA
SOUTH PACIFIC OCEAN
NEW ZEALAND

N

Acknowledgments

Certainly the stories and experiences in this book could not have been recorded and now memorialized for all time without my first being touched and encouraged by many wonderful and great people, many of whom were there as eyewitnesses and faithful recorders. Many, after hearing the stories over the years, expressed urgency that a written document be made as a reminder to the Niuean people of the faith and courage of their ancestors.

Chief among those "tormenters" (encouragers) were Shirley Bernice Motschman Goodman, my dear wife and loving companion of 46 years, and my dear children.

Chief among the eyewitnesses and recorders were H. Thayne Christensen and Thomas E. Slade, faithful missionary companions then and now; Jerry Ottley, who was in New Zealand at the time and provided document sources of mission president Sidney J. Ottley, his father; and Brother Fritz Bunge Krueger and his noble family, pioneers of the Church in the Pacific, who prepared and led the way.

Also acknowledged and appreciated, of course, are the Niuean Saints themselves, whom this historical record is about; my faithful, loving, and devoted brother in the gospel, Ikimautama Ikimau; and my dear sister and friend, Lagita Viliko Fakahoa, OBE, whom I will always esteem and remember as the *"Queen of Niue."*

Without the help and encouragement of all those mentioned above, this book would not have been possible. To them I am eternally grateful.

Although this book details history and events associated with The Church of Jesus Christ of Latter-day Saints, it is not an official publication of the Church. I assume full responsibility for the information contained herein.

Preface

FROM APRIL 1951 through January 1954, I served as a full-time missionary for The Church of Jesus Christ of Latter-day Saints. I was called to New Zealand and served one year there. Then I was transferred some 1500 miles northeast of New Zealand to the Polynesian island of Niue, where I served nearly two additional years. My experiences there changed my life.

In November 2000, I returned to Niue Island for the first time in 47 years. My dear wife, Shirley Bernice Motschman Goodman, accompanied me. During the 44 years of our marriage, I had told her about my unusual experiences as a young missionary in Niue, and I had tried to validate those events and impressions with stories, slides, photographs, and artifacts. But after the passing of so many years, my time in Niue seemed almost like a dream. Now Shirley would see the island for herself—and perhaps I would be able to relive with her some of the remarkable experiences I'd had there nearly half a century earlier.

Because of the unusual nature of my missionary experiences in Niue, I have decided to record them—not only for the benefit of our posterity, but also as a tribute to the beautiful Polynesian people of Niue. Their simple, transcendent faith clearly reveals them to be true children of the House of Israel.

Sources for this record include my own memory, journals and letters written by my mission president and companions, and other historical documents. (In quoted material, I have done some minor editing to maintain consistency in grammar, spelling, and punctuation.) The events as related are true as far as I can determine. As I look back now, nearly 50 years later, some of the events may seem incredible, but they did happen.

—Robert Maurice Goodman, 2002

One

A PRAYER OF FAITH

MY MISSIONARY COMPANION and I were preparing for a meeting in the village of Lakepa on the island of Niue when a woman rushed up to me. She was carrying a small boy who had been crying profusely. She asked if I would help comfort the child, and I said I would be happy to try. Then she extended her hand to give me something, and I opened my hand to receive it. Very gently she placed in the palm of my hand the severed forefinger of the young boy—apparently the finger had been cut off in an accident. With simple faith, she asked if I would please put the finger back on her son's hand and make it whole.

Never in all my life had I ever felt so totally humble, so completely inadequate, so absolutely helpless than at that moment. I stared down at the finger I was holding. "Could this finger be restored onto the hand of this little boy?" I wondered. "Do I have that much faith? And will the Lord grant that it should happen?" The longer I paused, the smaller I became within myself. The mother was waiting for my answer, and I needed to say something.

I quickly petitioned the Lord in silent prayer. A strong impression came that I should not attempt to restore the finger to its place on the child's hand but that I should bless him that he would never miss the finger and would live a long and useful life without it, never being hindered in his work because of its absence.

I explained to the mother the impression I had received, and she accepted it as God's will. Filled with faith, I proceeded to give her son the blessing, following the inspiration that had come to me.

Elders Reese Glines and Robert Goodman on the S.S. Aurangi, bound for New Zealand.

*Moumou and Elder Christensen,
August 1952*

In many ways, that event is symbolic of my experiences as a missionary in Niue. I was young and inexperienced. At times I wondered if I had enough faith to do what the Lord had called me to do. But my faith was strengthened by the simple yet profound faith of the Niuean people, whom I learned to love and cherish as my dear friends. And as my faith grew, I grew closer to the Lord and learned to trust in Him more fully.

When Shirley and I returned to Niue in 2000, we attempted to locate the nine-fingered boy, now a man. We were unsuccessful, but the search is not over. I am sure he has been blessed of the Lord, wherever he is.

Two

NIUE AS I KNEW IT IN 1952

ALTHOUGH IT IS NOT EASY to find Niue on the map, if you were to draw a line around all of Polynesia, including Hawaii and New Zealand, you would find Niue Island just about in the middle, at the very center of Polynesia. There is something about that tiny island that makes it different from all the rest of the world. Its location, physical characteristics, history, culture, and people make it unique even among other Polynesian islands.

When I visited Niue in 2000, I discovered that much had changed during the years since I had lived there as a missionary in the early 1950s. In 1959 and 1960, just a few short years after I left, two major cyclones hit the island with violent fury, destroying much of what I had known there. During the years of reconstruction that followed, many changes came to the island. Some of the old ways of doing things gave way to modern ways. For example, most of the wood and thached-roof huts were gone, replaced with new concrete structures. Some of the islanders gained access to defoliants and motorized farm equipment to work their plantations. And there was also a great surge toward political independence. In 1974 Niue became a self-governing state with an elected premier and a Legislative Assembly.

But the Niue of this story is the Niue of the early 1950's. Perhaps some background of the island and its people will provide a context. Some of the following details may seem boring or unnecessary, but I believe they are important to fully understand my experiences there.

Unloading tractor off S.S. Tofua in Alofi, 1953.

Where Is Niue?

Niue (pronounced "knee-oo-ay") is a sparkling, beautiful coral atoll island nation in the South Pacific that is seemingly lost among its more well-known neighbors, such as Tahiti (500 miles east), Samoa (300 miles north), Fiji (350 miles northwest), Tonga (240 miles west), and New Zealand (1500 miles southwest). Niue is located slightly northeast of the invisible intersection of the tropic of Capricorn and the international date line, at approximately 19° south latitude and 179° west longitude.

South view in rough seas.

Characteristics of the Land and Its People

Niue is one of the largest coral atolls in the world. Some people refer to the island simply as "the rock" or "the rock of Polynesia." This volcanic island has a total area of 100 square miles—about the size of Washington, D.C. It is 17 miles long and 10 miles wide at its widest point, and it has approximately 40 miles of rough coral roads.

The island has two terraced levels, one at 90 feet and the other at 200 feet above sea level. Unlike most of the rest of Polynesia, there are no sandy beaches in Niue. Steep, rugged cliffs of well-pounded coral rock form the shore line. There are very few places through these shear, unyielding black and gray cliffs where one can find access to the open sea. Small boats can dock at the wharf at the capital city of Alofi, and there are a few canoe landing places at such places as Avatele, Tuhia, and Uluvehi. But elsewhere, there are only a few deep, natural chasms, such as those at Vailoa and Matapa, through which one may reach sea level.

The harsh physical realities of the island have produced people of great courage and physical strength. To reap the harvest of the sea, the fishermen I knew in the 1950s first had to make their way down the steep cliffs, carrying canoes on their backs. Once they reached sea level, they had to brave the relentless heaving and pounding surf in order to get to the open sea. Too often one of our dear friends would go out to sea and never return. Stories of encounters with large fish, treacherous winds, driving currents, and ocean swells abounded among Niuean men. I believed those stories. I saw firsthand the courage and strength of Niuean fishermen.

Niuean farmers also had to have great courage and perseverance. The entire island is solid rock, covered by only a thin layer of soil in which to grow crops. In some places, farmers had to create individual seed holes at an angle so there would be enough soil to cover the seed plant. Because there are no lakes or rivers on the island, people would collect the rainwater that fell onto their tin roofs and store it in barrels or tanks (cisterns) for future use.

Despite these difficult conditions, families coaxed enough food from the soil and caught enough fish from the sea to sustain life. They were even able to export some items, such as bananas, taro (a starchy tuberous rootstock), and copra (dried coconut meat that yields coconut oil). The tropical climate was favorable for bounteous harvests, as long as it rained. During the summer (December through March) the average daytime temperature was about 82° F. During the winter (June through September) the average daytime temperature was about 72° F. Although droughts were frequent, and destructive cyclones hit Niue every few years, the trees and foliage of the island were usually lush and plentiful. There were many coconut, banana, and papaya trees, along with many exotic hardwoods. Before tractors and defoliants, Niueans cleared the land with bush knives and controlled fires.

The women of Niue were strong, resourceful, and hardworking. They worked the land alongside their husbands and taught their children at an early age the value and necessity of work. Niuean women were also famous for their many valuable, distinctive woven handicrafts made of native materials—especially the long, thin leaves (about four to five feet

A basket weaving contest among school girls in Alofi.

long) of the *fa* (pandus) tree. These handwoven items included baskets, hats, mats, fans, tapa cloth (a coarse cloth made of pounded bark and decorated with geometric patterns), and a host of other goods. Coconuts were also used in many of their creations.

Niueans had a reputation for their hard work, independent spirit, and courage to meet challenges and to defend what is theirs. In the 1950 edition of the *Pacific Island Year Book*, Niueans were described as "somewhat different in character from other Polynesians. They are very industrious and are keen traders. They are very much in demand as laborers. They are a rather remarkable section of the Polynesians." This was certainly my experience with them. The word in the South Pacific during the early 1950s was that if there was a task to be done and good, hardworking, dedicated, loyal workers were needed, Niue was the first place to look.

For sale—Niuean handicrafts on "boat day" in Alofi.

Niueans have their own eloquent Polynesian language and have fought to keep it alive. The fact that their language has survived the modernization of the past half-century says something about their tenacity. Most adults now speak English as well as Niuean, and English is the language of business and government on the island. But Niuean is still spoken at home, in school, and at social events. Niuean was the language of the island I knew as a missionary.

Early Inhabitants

Immigrants from Samoa and Tonga settled the island in approximately 500 A.D. to 1000 A.D. The first *patuiki* (king, or head chief) rose to power in 1600 A.D. He was followed by a series of kings, whose ruling councils consisted of chiefs and elders in each of the 12 villages on the island. The last king, Togia, died in 1917.

Captain Cook Visits Niue and Names It "Savage Island"

The unique nature of the Niuean people first evidenced itself historically when Captain James Cook (1728–79), the famous English navigator and explorer, attempted to land at Tuapa Cove and later did land near Opaahi on 20 June 1744. According to Niuean oral history, Captain Cook and his crew were fully armed with muskets, swords, and body armor; they were obviously ready for battle. But they were rebuffed by the Niueans, who with painted faces who threw spears, stones, and darts at them—one reportedly nearly hitting the great explorer himself. Captain Cook and his expedition retreated and declared that the people were savages. Thus for more than 200 years, the island was known as Savage Island, hardly an accurate description.

In not allowing Captain Cook to land on their island, the Niuean people were simply protecting their homes and families. The inhabitants of other islands weren't so fortunate. As historian Dick Scott observed: "Niueans were wise to guard their landing places from the pale aliens. At Tonga, where the white sails had just been, and at Tahiti, where they were next to go, a trusting welcome was repaid with much cruelty. Tongans were flogged with 30, 40, even 60 lashes for such 'insolence' as objecting to the felling of their trees. And although the Admiralty limit for Cook's sailors was a dozen lashes at one time, the leader of a Tongan, group who stoned persistent tree fellers received six dozen lashes—then Cook ordered that a cross be cut to the bone on both shoulders as a permanent reminder of British might. The lash was equally busy in Tahiti, houses were fired, and one thief had both ears cut off. The great explorer's violent death in Hawaii was not without reason" (Dick Scott, *Would a Good Man Die? Niue Island, New Zealand and the Late Mr Larsen*, Auckland, New Zealand: Hodder & Stoughton, Southern Cross Books).

The object of Captain Cook's expedition was obviously more for conquest than just for exploration. It is ironic that simple island people who fought against the captain's savagery would, themselves, be known as savages for more than 200 years. The 1950 Pacific Island Yearbook still identified Niue as "Savage Island."

The Arrival of Christianity

During the rule of the early kings, the religion on the island was apparently a pagan worship of the natural environment and the things in it, such as the sun, moon, large rocks, and large fish. Then in 1846, a Niuean named Peniamina (Benjamin), who had been converted to Christianity in Samoa, brought Christianity to his home island. He was joined three years later by a Samoan missionary named Paulo (Paul). These two Polynesian missionaries converted many people and spread Christianity and peace throughout the island.

Pre-Christian traditions, particularly among the chiefs of the village of Mutulau, spoke of a time when a man would come and teach of one God and would present it to them from a small book. Niueans looked forward to the fulfillment of this prophecy. When the Bible was first presented to the people of Mutulau, the entire village was converted to Christianity. From there the good word of God, as found in the Bible, spread throughout the island.

The Arrival of Europeans

In 1861, nearly 16 years after Peniamina had brought Christianity to Niue, the first *palagi* (white) missionary, Dr. George Lawes, arrived. In addition to bringing the Christian gospel, he and other missionaries who followed introduced aspects of the European way of life, such as Western-style clothing, commodities, culture, and economy.

There is little question concerning the good those early Christian missionaries of the London Missionary Society (LMS) accomplished. They helped strengthen the knowledge of the gospel of Jesus Christ, which Peniamina and Paulo had previously brought to Niue. They commissioned the Bible to be translated into the Niuean language. They taught the Niuean people to live the Ten Commandments and other gospel principles found in the New Testament. They taught the people to keep the Sabbath day holy. They helped establish Christian ethics and produced a relatively peaceful society. They did much to help the Niueans become humble, peaceful, God-fearing, Christian people. The early Christian missionaries were also helpful in organizing and writing the laws of the land; the first written laws of Niue were formulated by the Rev. F. E. Lawes in 1875.

In 1900, in response to the Niuean king's third request, Niue was proclaimed a British protectorate by Basil Thomson, envoy plenipotentiary. Lord Ranfurly, governor of New Zealand, visited Niue and formally annexed the island as a territory of New Zealand.

In 1901, the first British resident agent, Mr. S. Percy Smith, arrived. Two years later, the status of resident agent was upgraded to that of resident commissioner, and Mr. C. F. Maxwell was appointed to that position in 1903. (For a detailed historical perspective, see Edwin M. Loeb, *History and Traditions of Niue*, Honolulu, Hawaii: Bernice P. Bishop Museum, bulletin 32, 1926.)

Balance of Power

While the London Missionary Society did much to improve the lives of the inhabitants of Niue by teaching Christian ethics and values, the missionaries of the society also exercised a great deal of political control. In the early days of the Niuean kings, the native monarchy had governed the island. After the *palagi* missionaries took up residence, however, the power to rule developed into a joint-rule situation between the king and the LMS missionaries. In fact, the missionaries took such a major part in government that they greatly diminished the role of the king and his council. It is not clear why the king would request British involvement, but many suppose that the European missionaries' control over the people had made it almost impossible for the king to rule the island.

Mention of this ecclesiastical involvement in government was made as early as 1877. Loeb's *History and Traditions of Niue*, published in 1926, points out that "Mr. (Rev. F. E.) Lawes . . . was the virtual ruler over Niue" (page 42).

When Niue became a British protectorate, the Niuean king lost even more power and essentially became a figurehead. Togia, the last Niuean king, died in 1917. That left the LMS missionaries with even greater power and influence.

The control of the London Missionary Society became almost absolute on the island, and the head pastor began to rule much like a king. He had pastors in each of the 12 villages who, in essence, were his own council or tribunal.

For more than 90 years, the London Missionary Society was able to keep all other religions off the island. Some of the methods used to maintain this strong hold on the people were community ostracism, excommunication, stonings, and spiritual cursings. All of these actions created fear among the otherwise fearless Niuean people. Because they lived so close to nature and had to rely upon its bounty to provide, the people were anxious to please the god of nature. When a spiritual leader issued a curse or condemnation on someone, the people would take it very seriously. The practice of issuing curses and condemnations became a way of maintaining control over the people.

According to letters to the editor that were published in the *Aukland Times*, the rationale for allowing only one religion to exist in this otherwise free society was that a lack of freedom of religion enabled the people to live in peace and unity. However, the result was that there was no room

A typical Niuean hut.

Center of Alofi village during holiday fiafia

for expansion or exploration of ideas. In fact, the people lived in fear of anything beyond what was offered by the head pastor.

From my experience in Niue, I learned that there is a great problem in the making when a group tries, in a free society, to combine church and state to administer the affairs of government. Freedom of religion is one of the most basic tenets in a free society.

The resident commissioners, who represented the British Empire, had great difficulty in trying to administer the affairs of government. They found that they had to get permission or acquiescence from the LMS missionaries in order to administer the affairs of the island. They endured the system in order to keep the peace.

When I first arrived in Niue in 1952, I found that the London Missionary Society had been on the island for more than 90 years. When we advised the British resident commissioner of our desire to proselyte on the island, he welcomed us with open arms and a promise to help in any way he could. Indeed, Commissioner Cecil Hector Larsen became one of our closest friends, even though his position limited what he could do for us. We soon learned why he welcomed us so warmly.

Three

TO NEW ZEALAND—AND THEN TO NIUE

I RECEIVED MY CALL to serve as a missionary for The Church of Jesus Christ of Latter-day Saints on 3 April 1951. The letter was signed by George Albert Smith, the President of the Church. The very next day, President Smith passed away at the age of 81. Six days later, on 9 April 1951, David O. McKay was sustained as President of the Church at the age of 77. Thus my calling as a missionary began at approximately the same time as President McKay's calling as President.

My mission call stated that I was to serve in New Zealand for two years. I was thrilled with the assignment and tried to visualize myself in that faraway land. I had no reason to suppose I would actually serve there for only a year and would then be asked to extend my mission in order to help begin full-time missionary work on the tiny island of Niue. I had heard of New Zealand before, but I had never heard of Niue Island—nor would I until months later.

When I received my call, I was 21 years old, had just completed three years of service in the United States Air Force, and was living with my family in Washington, D.C. We were poor and had no financial resources to pay for my mission. My bishop, Joseph H. Tibbitts of the Capital Ward, explained the situation to our stake president, J. Willard Marriott Sr. of the Washington D.C. Stake. President Marriott and members of the stake high council decided to support me financially on my mission. I shall always be grateful to these good brethren for their assistance.

After I arrived at the mission home in Salt Lake City, Utah, Elder Bruce R. McConkie, then a member of the First Council of the Seventy, set me apart as a full-time missionary.

Voyage to New Zealand

On 3 May 1951—exactly one month after I received my call, and one day before my 22nd birthday—I left the port of Vancouver, Canada, on the cruise ship *S.S. Aorangi* of the Cunard Line, bound for New Zealand. Four other Latter-day Saint missionaries on board were also heading for New Zealand.

Elders Reese Glines and Robert Goodman on the S.S. Aurangi, bound for New Zealand.

On our second night out, I encountered my first blind prejudice concerning the Church. When we sat at dinner with some of the other passengers, we began to introduce ourselves and tell something about our business, as was the custom on cruise ships at the time. One by one, each person around the table gave a brief introduction. Then my turn came around. Since I was the first of the five missionaries to speak, I was happy to explain to this captive audience that we were Mormon missionaries on our way to New Zealand to do missionary work for the next two years.

At that moment all conversation stopped. There was dead silence. Across the table, an elderly lady, who was apparently very wealthy, sat for a few moments with her mouth agape. Then in a high-pitched tone and a very proper British accent, she said, "Oh my goodness, goodness gracious. I know why you are going to New Zealand." She turned to her companions and, in a completely serious tone of voice, explained: "When I was a small girl, my mother used to hide me under the bed any time she saw the

Mormon missionaries coming down the road. She told me that the objective of these missionaries was to get women and store them in that temple in Salt Lake City!"

It was my turn to be shocked. "She can't be serious," I thought. But it was obvious that she *was* serious. I decided to help her see how absurd her claim was. In a mock-serious tone, I answered: "Yes, ma'am, you are right. My quota is to get 25 women to store up in the Salt Lake Temple. If I do that, I will have had a successful mission!" Then, with a laugh, I added: "Keep in mind that there are more than 10,000 missionaries worldwide and that the temple is a building about 120 feet by 210 feet. Tell me—if we are all successful, where will we store all those 250,000 women?"

As I embellished this ridiculous scenario, others around the table began to join in, and we all began to laugh—including this dear English lady, who had carried a prejudice against Mormon missionaries all her life. We became friends with her that evening and during the rest of the cruise. But she wasn't quite ready for the gospel. It's amazing how prejudice doesn't allow us to be too concerned about the facts.

My First Missionary Assignment

After a voyage of about 21 days, we arrived in New Zealand. At that time, there were approximately 10,000 Church members in New Zealand. No stakes had been organized there yet. The entire Church organization was administered by the mission president, Gordon B. Young, who also presided over 100 full-time missionaries. Soon after my arrival, President Young called me to take charge of all the mission Sunday Schools and Mutual Improvement Associations (MIA, the forerunner of the Young Men and Young Women organizations) in New Zealand. I held this position throughout my first year of missionary service.

A New Mission President

In approximately December 1951, President Young completed his mission and was replaced by President Sidney J. Ottley of Salt Lake City. President Ottley was surely one of the great mission presidents of the Church. He loved the Lord and served with all his strength and energy, which seemed to be without end. He had a great sense of humor that helped us through the rough spots, which also seemed to be without end. He had sincere, deep love for the Saints and for all the people of New Zealand and neighboring islands. He was fearless in preaching the gospel and promoting the cause of Jesus Christ. A powerful instrument in the hand of the Lord, he helped the people live the gospel, laid the groundwork for the organization of stakes, started the construction of the New Zealand Temple, and extended the preaching of the gospel farther into the islands of the sea. During his tenure, his presidency covered not only the two islands of New Zealand, but also the Cook Islands, the Fijian Islands, and Niue Island.

We all learned to love and trust President Ottley. I relied heavily upon his love and trust in the months to come. He never once wavered or let us down. He was our good and dear friend.

President Sidney J. Ottley (center) with some missionaries outside the mission home, Auckland 1952.

Jerold D. Ottley, Son of President Ottley

When President and Sister Sidney J. Ottley arrived in New Zealand in October 1951 to begin their mission presidency, they brought with them the youngest of their six children, Jerold D. Ottley. Jerry, who was 17 at the time, became a significant help to his father and the work of the New Zealand Mission.

One of the great contributions the Ottleys made was directing the start of construction on the New Zealand College of The Church of Jesus Christ of Latter-day Saints in Hamilton. Thirty buildings were to be constructed on the 215 acre tract. Fifteen were under construction in July 1953. The Church sent Elder George R. Biesinger to direct the construction as project manager. Elder Biesinger was called as first councilor in the mission presidency to President Ottley.

Jerry worked for one full year as a labor missionary at the college, alongside many of the good Maori and Pakeha Saints. His work was hard physical labor. He also handled and inventoried tools, had responsibility to feed the pigs, and was later given the charge of keeping the construction accounting records.

Things would change for Jerry when he reached his 19th birthday. In his letter to me of 10 April 1953, President Ottley wrote: "We have ordained Jerry an elder and he will go into the [mission] field [in New Zealand] as soon as Elder Biesinger can arrange for someone to take over the books at the College."

Jerry served an honorable two-year proselyting mission in New Zealand. This gave him a total of four years of residence and service in New Zealand. He was released in July 1955, six months after his father and mother had returned home from their very successful mission.

Jerry went on to accomplish many wonderful things in his life. He earned his doctor of musical arts degree and was appointed by the First Presidency to become director of the world-renowned Mormon Tabernacle Choir, which position he held for 24 years until his retirement in 1999.

The Work Begins in Niue

I first heard of Niue Island from Brother Fritz Bunge Krueger of Samoa. This good and faithful member loved the Lord and desired to see the work of the Church move forward in the islands of the South Pacific. He had previously been instrumental in restarting missionary work on the island of Rarotonga in the Cook Island group. Now Brother Krueger asked President Ottley if he could initiate missionary work in Niue. He said he was willing to move to Niue with his wife and six small children to see if the island was ready for the preaching of the gospel. He would make his livelihood by showing motion pictures around the island, along with running a side business of baking bread. President Ottley responded favorably to Brother Krueger's noble desire and set him apart as a local missionary to accomplish that very purpose.

A document titled "A Brief History of the Church in Niue," stored in the mission home at Alofi, Niue, notes that on 22 January 1952, "Brother Fritz B. Krueger was set apart by President Sidney J. Ottley of N.Z. Mission to do missionary work on Niue Island. Not long after that Brother Krueger and his wife, Sister Isabel Krueger, with their young family of six girls arrived on Niue. They are the very first members of The Church of Jesus Christ Latter-day Saints to walk the soil of Niue."

During their eight short months on the island, beginning in February 1952, Brother Krueger and his family did many wonderful works to help start the Church there. As they traveled around the island showing movies and making bread, they became friends with many people. And they invited their friends and neighbors to hear, for the first time, the message of the Restoration. They started holding a home Sunday School, with their own little family leading the way.

Knowing that there would be great opposition, but feeling that there was an opportunity for missionary work to go forward in Niue, Brother Krueger contacted President Ottley, requesting that full-time missionaries be sent to the island.

Called to Niue

In March or April of 1952, President Ottley asked me if I would be willing to extend my mission and go to Niue Island to start the Church there. Of course, I was excited for the opportunity and told him I was ready to go at any time. President Ottley called Elder Wallace L. Barrett to be my companion. Elder Barrett had been working in the mission home and serving as the editor of the mission magazine, *Te Karere*.

Finding Out about Niue

To prepare ourselves for our new assignment, Elder Barrett and I excitedly gathered as much information as we could find. We learned some interesting things about Niue. First, we were going to a country with a language that was unfamiliar to us. It would be quite different from the Maori language we had been studying and speaking for a year. And there was little or nothing available to help us to become acquainted with the Niuean language.

Second, we were going to an island in a very remote area in the South Pacific, located some 1500 miles from mission headquarters in Auckland. Not only was Niue Island remote, but its only contact with the rest of the world was the visit of one ship per month—the *Tofua*—a small freighter that traveled between islands. Because there were no real harbors or docks on Niue, the freighter had to anchor offshore while the crew transferred the cargo onto lighters—small boats powered by oars and towed ashore by a small launch—that would transport the cargo to shore. When the sea was rough, which happened often during hurricane season (the first three months of the year), the *Tofua* would be unable to stop at Niue. It would continue its journey without stopping at Niue—and would not return until the following month.

We also learned that there were no airstrips of any kind and no radio stations. With the right equipment we could get some overseas shortwave radio reception. The Niuean government had shortwave radio communication with New Zealand. And telegraphed messages could be sent and received. But there were no electrical systems, no water supply systems, and no sewage systems. There was one crank-type telephone in each village, usually at the home of the police constable.

Stopover in Suva, Fiji

In order to catch up with the *Tofua*, which had already started on its rounds, Elder Barrett and I flew by airboat to Suva, Fiji. There we had to wait a few days for the *Tofua* to leave for Niue, so we had an opportunity to explore Suva.

At that time, approximately half of the population of the Fiji Islands were of Polynesian descent. The other half were of East Indian descent— mostly from India itself—and of the Hindu religion. The country was a colony of the British Crown.

We stopped at a "milk bar," thinking we might be able to buy some ice cream. Each of us ordered a banana split. As we waited for our order to arrive, we envisioned the great feast we were about to enjoy. We knew we were in the land of bananas, where you could buy a whole stalk for one shilling—about 15¢. But to our surprise and disappointment, the young woman who served us took one banana, cut it in half, placed one half on Elder Barrett's dessert plate, and placed the other half on mine! And she scooped only a small amount of ice cream onto each banana half. Elder Barrett, a real banana lover, was devastated. After we had

Above: Elder Goodman (left) and Elder Barrett boarding airboat (inset).

23

eaten our scanty treat, he walked over to the young woman and asked, "If I had come in by myself and ordered a banana split, what would you have done with the other half of the banana?" I don't think he got an answer, but at least he had the satisfaction of asking.

While in Fiji we visited a Hindu tailor, who took our measurements and made us white linen suits, the type that were usually worn in the tropics at that time. Each of us was pleased with the results: The fit was good, the price was very inexpensive, and the workmanship was excellent.

President Ottley joined us in Suva to await the departure of the *Tofua*. Two members of the Church from Samoa—Tavita Fitisemu, the chief of police, and his wife—also joined us. They were going to travel on the *Tofua* back to their home in Samoa. We greatly enjoyed their company.

President Ottley and Elder Goodman in the marketplace, Suva, Fiji.

When Sunday came, we began looking for a place to hold a sacrament meeting. We did not know of any other members of the Church in Fiji at that time, and we wondered if a Latter-day Saint sacrament meeting had ever been held in Fiji. We asked our taxi driver—a man of East Indian ancestry who had been showing us around—where we might hold our meeting. He thought for a minute and said he did not know of a place. But then he surprised us by saying, "I would be happy to have you come to my home."

Of course, we were delighted, and we accepted his generous offer with sincere gratitude. We were excited about the prospect of sharing tenets of our faith with this sincere, humble Hindu man and his family.

When we arrived at his humble home with cement walls and a tin roof, our gracious host immediately invited us in and introduced us to his wife and four young children. Although they seemed surprised at our visit, they welcomed us and made us feel comfortable. (I do not remember our host's name, but I have a picture of him and his family.) As we sat on the floor to start our meeting, we realized that the only partitions in the one-roomed home were paisley-patterned cloths hanging from the ceiling.

First Sacrament meeting in Fiji at home of Hindu cab driver (man at right).

We also realized that we had no bread for the sacrament. Our host said he didn't have any bread, so we began looking around for a substitute. Looking out the window, we spotted a breadfruit tree, and we picked some of its fruit to use for the sacrament. We figured the Lord would not mind, as long as we got the prayers right and had the right attitude.

That simple sacrament meeting in the humble home of our gracious Hindu host was one I will never forget. There seemed to be an extra portion of the Lord's Spirit with us that day as we offered the sacrament prayers, partook of the sacrament, and testified of our blessings. Each of us—Brother and Sister Fitisemu, President Ottley, Elder Barrett, and I—felt the significance of participating in what was perhaps the first Latter-day Saint sacrament meeting in Fiji.

Whether it was actually the first LDS sacrament meeting in Fiji or not didn't really matter to us. Perhaps some members of the Allied troops who had been in or near Fiji during World War II had held a sacrament meeting there. We felt it significant, however, that several months after our meeting in the taxi driver's home, the First Presidency directed President Ottley to organize the Church in Fiji and to administer it under the New Zealand Mission. In a letter to me, dated 5 May 1953, President Ottley wrote: "I have the commission from the First Presidency to hunt up all the members in that city [Suva, Fiji] and assume responsibility of the organization of them and they will become part of the New Zealand Mission instead of Tongan." Less than 50 years later, in 2001, there were more than 12,000 members of the Church in Fiji—and a temple, which was dedicated on 18 June 2000.

Aboard the Tofua

At last we boarded the *Tofua* and began our long-awaited journey to Niue. (See Entry Permit, my offical pass to enter and leave Niue, Appendix A.) As we sailed, it occurred to us that we had no housing arrangements on the island. The Kruegers certainly couldn't accommodate us in their large family's small living quarters, and there were no hotels on the island. We were traveling on faith, trusting that the Lord would provide. As Nephi wrote, we were being "led by the Spirit, not knowing beforehand the things which [we] should do" (1 Nephi 4:6).

Boarding the S.S. Tofua at Suva, Fiji, bound for Niue.

In addition to wondering where we would stay, we also wondered how we would be received. Since the sole religion on Niue had been able to keep all other religions off the island for 107 years, we knew our welcoming committee would be lacking some gusto.

The Colorful Captain Bell

The Lord rewarded us for our trust in Him. On the ship, we met an elderly gentleman. Captain William Moody Bell, a retired British army officer, owned the Niue Island Trading Company and was returning to the island to take care of some business. Years earlier, he had been the resident commissioner on Niue Island—the representative of the British government. Although he had been rather controversial during his time as resident commissioner, he knew the island and the people well, and he knew how to do things on Niue.

In answer to our prayers, we learned that Captain Bell owned some vacant rooms behind his trading store. Through President Ottley, he offered the rooms to us, and we gladly accepted. We were happy to know we would have a place to stay when we got to the island.

Captain Bell was the personification of a typical retired British army officer and gentleman. During our association with him, we learned to like his stiff, yet kind, ramrod military manner and his heavy British accent. He dressed in summer military khaki clothing, wore boots and a pith helmet, and sported a full gray Pancho Villa-type mustache. He and President Ottley became good friends and communicated often. He was a friend to the Church. I was saddened to learn that he died in 1954 at the age of 75—only a couple of years after we met him on the *Tofua*.

A Question Never to Be Forgotten

During our voyage to Niue, we became friendly with many of the crew members and were able to get around the old *Tofua* pretty well.

The S.S. *Tofua* leaving Auckland.

Approaching Alofi—a view from the bridge of the S.S. Tofua.

When we explained our mission to the crew, they said they thought we would have a hard time accomplishing it.

As we finally approached the island of Niue, we were allowed to go up to the bridge for a better look. While I was gazing at the island, which was still some distance away, one of the officers asked me a question that I have never forgotten. "Elder Goodman," he said, "knowing that these people have had one single religion for more than 90 years and have lived in peace and harmony with it, why do you want to bring disunity and contention among them?"

Lighter being towed ashore from the Tofua.

The officer's question surprised and disconcerted me. I knew why we were going to Niue, but I didn't have enough time to help him understand the eternal significance of our mission. It seemed that the question was designed to give me serious personal doubts about what we were going to do and why. The question was loaded with innuendo—yet it had an element of truth in it. I knew that was Satan's way, and I wondered if Satan was trying to plant a seed of doubt and uncertainty in my mind before I had even stepped foot on Niue's soil.

I reminded myself that I would never wish to bring disharmony or harm of any kind to Heavenly Father's children on Niue. In fact my objectives were quite the opposite. My mission was to help fulfill ancient and modern scripture that the people of the islands of the sea would be

Our welcoming party upon our arrival in Niue (from left): Sister Fitisemanu, Sister Krueger and children, Sister (unknown), Brother Fitisemanu, Elder Barrett, Brother (unknown), Brother (unknown), President Ottley, and Fritz Krueger.

made aware of the workings of God in these latter days. They needed to know that God had spoken again and had given us another testament of Jesus Christ—the Book of Mormon. They needed to know of the restored priesthood power and have the opportunity to receive the ordinances of salvation.

I am not sure what answer I gave to the officer on the *Tofua* that day. I think I merely said that we had a message to deliver and that we were going to do it. But his question stayed with me for some time.

On 10 May 1952, President Ottley, Elder Barrett, and I landed on Niue Island.

Four

BEGINNING THE WORK ON NIUE

AFTER A LONG VOYAGE we were glad to be on terra firma. We were especially excited to have finally reached "the Rock," as Niue is affectionately called and adequately described. In the main village of Alofi, Brother Fritz Krueger and his family were ecstatic to see us—and we them. After greetings, *kai* (food), and some visiting, we proceeded with the work at hand.

President Ottley had several reasons for coming with us to Niue. During the few hours the *Tofua* was being unloaded, he wanted to see the island for himself, visit the Kruegers, see to it that we got settled, and give me the charge as district president. Most important, he wanted to dedicate the island for the preaching of the gospel. Then, after a few short hours with us on the island, he would return on the *Tofua* to New Zealand.

Niue Island Dedicated for the Teaching of the Gospel

And so it was that on 10 May 1952, President Sidney J. Ottley dedicated Niue Island for the preaching of the restored gospel of Jesus Christ. As I remember it, the dedicatory prayer was forthright and simple. Through the power of the Melchizedek Priesthood and by the authority he held, President Ottley called for the powers of heaven to be present. He blessed us as missionaries that we would be protected and strengthened as we proceeded with this great work. He blessed the people that their minds and hearts would be opened. He prayed that the island would be blessed, that peace would prevail, and that a way would be opened for the work to go forward.

Young man collecting uga (large coconut land crabs) in thick bush.

The dedicatory service was simple, mostly private, and carried out without much fanfare. Yet it was done with sincere faith, with deep humility, and with great eloquence that characterized President Ottley in all he did. We then went to look at our new quarters at Anakale.

Anakale, "Cave of the Birds"

The rooms Captain Bell had offered us turned out to be sort of a lean-to attached to the back of a small, little-used store. There were two small rooms, non-adjoining, each with entrances from the outside. We used one of the rooms for sleeping and the other for preparing food and washing up. There were no windows, just openings where windows could be placed. The doors were very fragile; they had no outside locks and the bottom edge of the doors did not reach the floor. The toilet was a wooden outhouse several yards away.

Our water supply came from an outside water tank (cistern) that caught the rainwater from the rusty metal roof. We had no refrigerator or sink, only a small kerosene camping stove to cook on. We ate mostly out of cans. We had a small table with a couple of chairs, and we slept on rope-threaded cots under mosquito nets.

Anakale, our first home in Niue. Elder Goodman gives Elder Barrett a haircut. Notice newly fashioned broom handle and cisterns for water.

Elder Goodman holds an uga, the large land coconut crab of Niue. Notice how the tail resembles a lobster.

As humble as it was, we were thankful to have something. This was our home—Anakale, "the cave of the birds." We called it simply "the cave."

What's for Lunch?

In addition to the fruit on the trees and the fish in the sea, there were many other good natural food sources on the island. There were also wild and domestic pigs and chickens. And a wonderful meal could be had from the land crabs that seemed to be everywhere.

The *uga* (oo-nga) is a delicious dish comparable to king crab. It is a large crab; with its claws outstretched, it can grow as big as two to three feet long. It is an unusual land crab that lives on coconuts. It climbs up the coconut tree backwards, snips off a coconut with its pinchers, climbs back down the tree, and proceeds to take the coconut apart with its powerful claws. If you have ever tried to open a fresh coconut, you know that it takes a great amount of strength to do so.

Kalehimus are small land crabs; you need a lot of them to make a good meal. They live in the coral rock and make themselves a nuisance

Niue's peka flying fox (large bat-like animals).

when it rains because they seem to want to seek shelter wherever they can find it. We found that after rainstorms, many of them usually ended up all over our little quarters, especially in our shoes and bedding.

The *peka* (flying fox or fruit bat) was a food source that we didn't care much for. They dwell in caves and trees. Some have a wing span about three feet long.

Easy Fishing, Thanks to the Kieto Tree

Every August, when the red berries of the *kieto* tree are fully ripe, the Niueans would take them and cast them into the sea near the shore at the

Stunning fish with kieto berries near Alofi.

A blow fish captured when fish were stunned by kieto berries.

Alofi wharf. Apparently the red berry had a stunning affect on the fish, making them listless, slow, and very easy to catch or spear. The water in the area took on a red color.

People would gather in large numbers and ceremoniously begin this easy harvest from the sea. They would go into the water at low tide and, while walking on the sharp coral rock, gather as many of the fish as possible. The whole process had to be completed before the next high tide. It was a beautiful sight to see.

I think many Niueans felt this was God's way of helping them occasionally with an otherwise difficult and dangerous chore. It is my understanding that this activity is no longer done on Niue.

Ready to Start the Work

After his few hours on the island, President Ottley left on the *Tofua*. We were sad to see him go, but we were ready to get started. We spent much of the next few days and weeks with Brother Fritz Krueger and his family, getting to know them and preparing to continue on with their work. They were a noble family who were trying to do the Lord's work in a remote area of the world. We learned to love and appreciate them very much. Even though Fritz had to spend much of his time making a living to support his family in this very poor area, he gave us all the strength he had. He was a great help to us as we set about meeting and getting to know the people.

Beginning Our Work

There were very few motor vehicles on the island. Neither we nor Brother Krueger were privileged to have one. In fact, we did not even have bicycles until many months later. Therefore, all of our work was centered in the main village of Alofi.

Expanding on the efforts Brother Krueger had begun, we began our work by gathering in more people who were interested and curious. The only way we could communicate with some of the people was by using plain and simple illustrations that could transcend language differences. Fortunately, however, there were some young native boys and girls among our group who were familiar enough with the English language to act as translators for us. With their help, and by learning a few key words and phrases, we were able to communicate somewhat.

Our first lessons were to show these children of God that we were interested in them. We had come with a message of love and hope from a prophet of God. We began our efforts by doing many fun activities that

Young man dressed for fiafia (Niuean dance) and Elder Goodman with guitar.

the people enjoyed. I had managed to bring along my old guitar, so we taught them to sing cowboy songs, and they taught us island songs.

Niue's First Volleyball Game

The first time the *Tofua* came with some mail for me, I received a "care" package from someone back home. One of the treasures in the package was a green rubber ball about the size of a volleyball. I went to one of the traders and purchased fishing line, from which I fashioned a volleyball net. We stretched the net in front of some houses (huts) in Alofi

The first volleyball game on Niue.

and started the first volleyball game ever on Niue. The young people loved it. Many of them become very friendly to us, particularly when we would sing and hold an MIA meeting or activity.

Teaching the Restoration

We started holding morning Sunday School meetings and Bible study classes at night. Later we started holding classes in which we taught more about the restored gospel of Jesus Christ, the First Vision, and the mission of the Prophet Joseph Smith. We took turns teaching. Brother Krueger was a good teacher and could communicate very well. He was, indeed, a great asset to the work.

More and more adults started to attend the classes and to join with their young people in our games and singing. Many seemed interested and eager to learn. As our little congregation grew to nearly 100 and continued growing, we began to look around for a more permanent place to hold our meetings.

The old Blue Bell—our first meeting place, Alofi, 1952.

The Blue Bell, Niue's First Meeting Place

At the south end of Alofi, less than a mile from the Krueger home, was a structure known as the Blue Bell Club. For years the Blue Bell had been used for dancing and other social activities. Now it was standing idle and seemed to be available. The owner of the building, Mr. Star Watch (Sita Uati), had attended many of our meetings, along with some of his family members. They were interested in what we were doing. Brother Krueger knew him and made inquiries, and Mr. Star Watch generously offered the use of the building to us at no cost. He later joined the Church and became one of the Lord's great servants. Brother Star was one of the early ones whom the Spirit inspired to help us move forward the Lord's work on Niue.

Sita Uati (Star Watch), 1952.

The Blue Bell was located at Lalosiale, Alofi South, overlooking the wide Pacific Ocean. The floor and foundation were concrete—about 30 feet by 30 feet. The frame of the building was made of wood, and the roof and sides were clad with corrugated iron sheets. Because of the building's location, it was vulnerable to the salt air, which created lots of rust. The windows were just openings, without shutters. The doorways were also

Our first congregation in Alofi. Unpainted Blue Bell at right.

just openings, without doors.

Rickety as the good old Blue Bell appeared to us spoiled "Yanks," it was beautiful to us as missionaries. It was a fine structure for us at the time. We loved being there with our dear new friends and watching their joy in learning more about the restored gospel. As was the custom at the time, we all sat on the floor on woven mats. Because there was no public electrical service, kerosene lamps were our only source of light after dark, except for an occasional flashlight.

Brother Ikimautama Ikimau, a dear Niuean friend and brother who was a young boy at the time, has provided much research and information for this record. He shares some of his childhood memories concerning the Blue Bell: "Blue Bell was one of the recognized and respected entertainment facilities of Niue. These facilities were used strictly for European type dancing such as the fox trot, waltz and others. Mr. and Mrs. Sita Uati were very professional with such steps. It was beautiful to watch. They were marvelous dancers. The band was of local men. [To create music] they used such items as the ukulele, the guitar, or anything else that was hollow and made a sound. For bass they used a 44-gallon drum, cut in half. One half was equipped with a pole and a string to create the bass sound. The music was sweet and fit in with the item steps. Inhaling of tobaccos and consuming the local beverage helped all of them enjoy the evening. Such mood gave us window peepers more fun and more laughs. . . .

"The Blue Bell was owned by Mr. Sita A. Uati and Mrs. Manhetule F. Uati. They too were the managers of the dancing club called 'Blue Bell' from its humble beginning to the end of its hey-days. Perhaps in the minds of Mr. and Mrs. Uati, allowing the hall to be used for church

. purposes was their dream come true. Instead of entertaining the physical body, it was now used to invite the divine Spirit to entertain the soul and satisfy the inner person. Mrs. Manhetule Fay Uati and one of their sons, Radio Safiu Uati, were among the very first group baptized in The Church of Jesus Christ of Latter-day Saints. They were among the first 26 members of the Church in Niue on 14 August 1952.

"Although Mr. Sita Avoki Uati did not join the Church at that time, he later followed his wife's footsteps and became one of the Church's stalwart members. He dedicated his life to promoting the interests of the gospel. He helped many of his friends, loved ones, and relatives join the Church."

The Blue Bell was now the official Church meeting place of Alofi and all of Niue Island. Here we conducted all our Church meetings and activities—Sunday School, sacrament and testimony meetings, and MIA activities. Here we taught the gospel to those spiritually prepared to receive and embrace it. Many people were converted to the Church from the lessons and activities they received in our beloved Blue Bell hall. These things were freely given and freely received in our rent-free premises. Only divine help made this possible. Those were wonderful and joyous times as we began to build the kingdom and unfold the great things ahead for these people.

We will forever remember the generosity of Brother and Sister Uati for allowing us to use their hall to conduct all our activities with no request for payment of any kind. There were no signed leases or deeds. Neither were there any conditions of how or when we could use the building or

Early Alofi congregation. Rangi and Solomona at right.

what we were allowed to do inside it. We were free to hold any activity we wished. They loved us and trusted us in the things we were doing. This demonstrates another great character trait of the Niuean people.

The Adversary Begins to Show

Of course, the adversary was busy working on our little congregation. Cursings—threats of dire consequences, including bodily harm and even death—were promised those who listened to the Mormon missionaries. A lot of these threats were coming from the pulpits of the other church as a means of maintaining control of the people. The use of cursing and predicting calamitous consequences was a common practice among this isolated people, who lived so close to nature and relied upon its sustenance.

This practice affected some of our little flock, but not many. The stalwarts, having received their testimonies from the Spirit, hung on. And we kept providing all the care we could. The Lord was certainly with us during this difficult time.

Our First Written "Message to Israel"

So prevalent were these abuses, that we decided to write and distribute a tract stating our position and objectives. We had an old typewriter and a spirit duplicator that enabled us to make copies of songs, tracts, lesson plans, and anything else we needed to print. We titled our first tract "A MESSAGE TO ISRAEL" (referring to the Niuean people), wrote it in both the English and Niuean languages, and distributed copies to all who would receive them. In the text of the tract, we quoted scriptures from the Bible, clarified points of doctrine, and explained who we were and why we were on Niue. Included in the message was the following paragraph commenting on the practice of cursing:

"Our Prophets and Apostles, with the guidance of the Lord, lead the Church with love and understanding, not with fear and with cursing. The Apostle Paul tells us to 'bless and curse not.' (See Romans 12:14.) God never meant that His children should be ruled with fear and with cursing. Jesus Christ gave His life to give us His gospel, and He did it with love not with the mighty power of God that He had." (A copy of the original letter is in our research files. See Appendix B for the full text.)

We don't think our tract changed the practice of cursing much; it still goes on today. I think, however, that we did win over some converts and also strengthened our own people.

Stonings and Elder Barrett

Stoning was another way that the opposition expressed itself. We joked among ourselves that the reason people threw stones at us was that stones were what they had the most of. Surely they did have many—and some people didn't mind using them, as we were to see in the months to come.

Probably the most difficult problem we had from stonings came one night during the first week of July 1952. As Elder Barrett and I were sleeping in our little place at Anakale, "cave of the birds," there suddenly came a thunderous hail of stones and rocks upon our tin roof. The racket was so terrible that we were sure our roof was going to cave in. We quickly pulled on some clothes and ran out into the night to hide in the bush. The attack quickly ceased, so we returned to our little home. We had not been hit or harmed in any way from the stones.

However, Elder Barrett had failed to put on his shoes, and he suffered severe cuts on his feet. Some of the coral rock outcroppings on Niue are poisonous—and Elder Barrett's wounded feet became badly infected. Over the next few days, his legs and body began swelling, and he was in serious pain. His eyes and nerves were also giving him great difficulty. The doctor did all he could, and we continually petitioned the Lord in Elder

The Tofua, loading and unloading on a calm sea.

Barrett's behalf. Our hearts went out to him as we did all we could to make him comfortable. But we knew he needed additional medical attention. We telegraphed this information to the mission home, and many people in New Zealand fasted and prayed for Elder Barrett.

It was a great blessing that the *Tofua* was due in only a few days. We arranged passage for him to go to Apia, Samoa, and to fly from there back to the mission home in New Zealand. From there he soon returned to the United States.

So it was that on 19 July 1952, Elder Wallace L. Barrett, a noble son who gave much to get the work started, left Niue Island. It was sad to see him leave. Later we were glad to hear that after receiving proper treatment, he was restored to his normal health. He remained in the United States.

As the *Tofua* carrying Elder Barrett disappeared over the horizon and the sun started to set, I went back to Anakale. I suddenly realized I was alone.

Five

OUR FIRST BAPTISMS

AFTER REALIZING I WAS ALONE—between the proverbial rock (Niue) and a hard place (the remote South Pacific Ocean)—I decided to ask Brother Wilson "Moumou" McMoore, one of the young Niuean men who had been friendly with us from the beginning, to take Elder Barrett's place at Anakale and be my temporary companion.

Because we had not yet held baptisms, there were not yet any members of the Church on Niue except for the Kruegers. But although Moumou was not a member of the Church, he was very willing and delighted to serve. He took part in most of our activities and seemed to enjoy them very much. He understood English well and was not afraid of the cursings of the other church. He was a little older than most of the other young men and was a little more serious about things. Besides all of that, he was a good cook! Moumou was a welcomed companion. He became my very good, close friend. I considered him to be one of the quiet blessings the Lord gave us to help the work continue.

Together, we carried on with our work. While Moumou kept busy helping us gather more people and establish greater friendships, Brother Krueger and I did the teaching. The *Tofua* that took Elder Barrett away also bought us bicycles from the mission home. Prior to that time, since we had no transportation, all of our work had been confined to the main village of Alofi. With the bicycles, we were able to begin teaching in five other villages. The work was progressing—and the stonings continued. Fortunately there were no serious incidents as a result.

Elder Goodman and his second (temporary) companion, Wilson "Moumou" McMoore.

Elder Christensen Arrives

The *Tofua* that arrived on 9 August 1952 brought Elder Horace Thayne Christensen to replace Elder Barrett as my companion. I was sincerely pleased to welcome him to Niue. I gave him a big, long hug—and then took an even bigger sigh of relief. He was slightly younger than I but was an experienced missionary, having worked in Nuhaka, Hawkes Bay, New Zealand, and other places. As history will show, Elder Christensen would

become one of the great missionaries of our day. He was a strong, dedicated companion who met every challenge cheerfully and with a willing heart. He loved the Lord and loved to teach the people.

Among Elder Christensen's many other contributions was his ability to keep records and make out our reports. All during his mission, Elder Christensen kept a personal journal. Two hundred and fifty pages cover his time on Niue. He has given me copies of those pages, along with permission to quote from them. They are invaluable in authenticating our story. (Quotes from Elder Christensen's journal will hereafter be cited as "ECJ.")

Elder Goodman greets Elder Christensen (right) on his arrival in Niue, August 1952.

Baptisms!

On 14 August 1952, five days after Elder Christensen arrived, a long-awaited event took place. We held our first baptismal service and baptized 26 people! What a wonderful time it was. The people were ready and eager. The Spirit had witnessed to them that the Church was true. Without fear and in the face of great persecution—the ranting, raging, and cursing of the other church and the rejection of their families and communities—they were ready to exercise the first principles and ordinances of the gospel: faith in the Lord Jesus Christ, repentance, baptism by immersion, and the gift of the Holy Ghost.

The courage, independence, and faith shown by these early Church members demonstrates another wonderful characteristic of the Niuean people. We greatly rejoiced with these, our new and dear friends. There was a wonderful outpouring of love for each other at that time. It still exists today.

First congregation of the Blue Bell, 1952.

The Amanau Cave

We knew we had to be careful while planning and carrying out the baptismal service. The intensity of the abuse on our people was increasing. The adversary seemed to be well informed of what was about to happen. I feel sure that he was trying to stop it.

We decided we would have to go at night after everything had settled down for the day. We hired a truck during the day, and that night we loaded everyone on board and went to the Amanau Cave, 1 1/2 miles south of Alofi.

When we reached the pathway to the cave, we left the truck at the side of the road and descended single file down the 100-foot coral cliff in the darkness. Our only light came from kerosene lanterns and a few flashlights. The Amanau Cave is at sea level, facing the open Pacific Ocean. The sea seemed quieter than usual. There wasn't the normal pounding surf nor the rolling incoming waves that otherwise seemed to be endless.

The pool inside the cave was calm and, as always, crystal clear. The light of the kerosene lanterns created beautiful cathedral-like patterns as they illuminated the walls and ceiling of the cave. Only the God of heaven could have produced such beautiful patterns in that natural setting. I felt that there could not have been in all the world a more beautiful and peaceful setting than in that cave on that night. Some others later wrote that there was more light present than that provided by our humble kerosene lanterns and flashlights. This I knew was true.

In the report I later sent to mission headquarters, I made a statement that has been used and often quoted when referring to this first baptism. Speaking of ourselves as missionaries, I wrote: "Our hearts were greatly moved, because we realized that their faith was pure." I knew their faith was pure because of their almost complete sacrifice of everything they had and their willingness to follow the Savior's admonition to repent and be baptized. Surely, the light of the Spirit of the Lord did shine in the hearts and on the faces of each of those noble sons and daughters of God. It was a pleasure to be in their presence.

I baptized 10 people, Brother Krueger baptized 10, and Elder Christensen baptized six. In our report to mission headquarters, we quot-

Elder Goodman and Kim at the mouth of the Amanau Cave.

ed Jeremiah 16:16: "Behold, I will send for many fishers, saith the Lord, and they shall fish them; and after will I send for many hunters, and they shall hunt them from every mountain, and from every hill, and out of the holes of the rocks." And I added the following note: "WE ARE THE HUNTERS!"

Elder Christensen wrote: "August 14, 1952: The angels will be rejoicing in heaven. . . . We baptized and confirmed 26 people as (the first Niuean) converts to the gospel of Jesus Christ. . . . It was wonderful to see the expressions on their faces after baptism. . . . It was a beautiful spot for a baptism" (ECJ, 302).

The 26 people who were baptized and confirmed on 14 August 1952 were:

ESETELA MOKO	FORTYONE MILANI
FUAMANOGI KULUIA	ATALINI KAUHEMOTU
KAUHEMOTU KAUHIVA	MOKALIGI TOHOVAKA
GLENICE M. KRUEGER	LAGITAFUKE (RANGI) FAKAHOA
MAIKA PEAUFA	MANAHETULE FAY UATI (WATCH)
MANOGIOGO MILANI	MEKISINA SIONO
TIVAEGA NASALITA OLIFE	ETEKATI PIUTI
PUNATAU MAHIKA OLIFE	RADIO SAFIU UATI (WATCH)
TOGIAONO	KAUHATUKI TASMANIA
HELI TAULAGAONOTAMA	MELEVALU TAULAGAONOTAMA
OLIFE TOGIAONO	TOMUHAPA VATU
WILLIAM	TALITOGIA ULINE OLIFI
TUFUGA PIUTI	JOHN VIA KOLO

Elder Christensen and Kim in the Amanau Cave pool.

More Trials

More trials were in store for these dear faithful people. But now, armed with the Spirit of the Lord and with firm determination, they would endure adversity well. Ugly rumors became rampant among the people that any government employee in Niue who joined the LDS Church would be fired. If this report had been true, it would have affected some of our people. But Resident Commissioner Larsen issued the following statement to all governmental departments:

"Owing to rumors now circulating among Niueans generally, several administration employees have expressed concern that their services as members of the staff might be terminated because of their religious beliefs. Please draw to the attention of all your staff immediately that employees of the administration are free to belong to any religious denomination they choose."

"Signed, Cecil Hector Watson Larsen, Resident Commissioner" (See Appendix C for a full copy of this letter.)

The Krueger Family Leaves

On 10 September 1952, just eight short months after their arrival, Brother and Sister Krueger and their family had to leave the island of Niue earlier than we had all expected. Their departure was caused by the slowness of business and the fact that Sister Krueger was ill. We felt a great void when this dear family left Niue.

Fritz Krueger and family and friends, on the day the Krueger family left Niue, September 1952.

Then on 19 December 1952, some 99 days later, we received a letter from Brother Krueger reporting that his wife, Isabel, had passed away. We all felt a deep, sincere loss at the passing of Sister Krueger and deep sympathy for Fritz and his young family.

More Baptisms

Now that a long trend of having only one church on the island had been broken, more people become interested in joining our little congregation. We soon held two more baptismal services in the Amanau Cave.

The 12 people who were baptized and confirmed on 28 August 1952 were:

HARRY AHOHAILE	LEA TAUFAKATATA
ROSALINA JACKSON	SOFINE LORRIMER SOLOMONA
VILIKO MALIKO FAKAHOA	NUASA TOGIAONO
OBEDIENT MILANI	SOLOMONA UKAMOTU
FANIVA SIFAKIKILA	TUAFALE
ALOMATAMA	FALAILE

The four males who were baptized and confirmed on 29 September 1952 were:

ASEKONA LUKUPA	MATAKIETO VALEPO
FOAHALA FOULAGI	LAGAVALU HAIOSI

These were the first 42 people baptized in Niue at Amanau Cave. Later there were many others baptized in other places around the island. However, these were the first. They became the strength from which we were able to go forward to the other villages. I shall always remember them, love them, and hold them in great regard because of their faith and courage.

"Get Off the Island or Else"

A few days after our second baptismal service, a note appeared on our door—the first of many similar notes we would receive. And, of course, the stonings continued. Elder Christensen wrote: "Aug. 29th, 1952: When we got up this morning we found a note . . . on our door that stated that if we didn't get off the island with our religion there would be some serious trouble. They didn't bother us any" (ECJ, 309).

"Sept. 2, 1952: This evening we biked out to Mutulau [which is 12 miles over the bumpiest road in the world] to hold a cottage meeting with the people. Our meeting was interrupted as several big stones were thrown at the house. [When we left,] the owner of the house biked a couple of miles out of town with us so that people wouldn't throw rocks at us [again]" (ECJ, 321).

During this time, a group of Niuean people came to us and said they wanted to be baptized—but they had not yet received the needed teaching and they had not studied and prayed. In the New Zealand Mission Historical Record is the following note I wrote on 3 October 1952 and sent to mission headquarters: "Since our arriving here we have had numerous requests for baptism. We are trying to exercise wisdom in the matter and assuring them baptism at a later date after they learn why they are being baptized. We feel this entirely necessary in order to glean the earnest converts from the malcontenders and people harboring ulterior motives. R. M. Goodman, District Pres."

Appointment As Marriage Officer
As district president, I began to receive requests to conduct other ecclesiastical duties, such as funerals and marriages. On 22 August 1952, Resident

One of the many weddings performed by Elder Goodman on Niue.

Commissioner Cecil H. Larsen gave me a "Warrant of Appointment" as a marriage officer on Niue. (See Appendix D for a copy of this document.) After receiving this official authorization from the government, I was able to perform marriages for some of our members and for others who were not. On 12 September 1952, I performed the marriage of Tuafale (a member) and Peneti of Alofi. A large *fiafia* was held in honor of the newlyweds, which we all enjoyed very much. Many other marriages followed.

A Second "Message to Israel"

At this point, we began working on our second "Message to Israel." This message was on the topic of baptism. The other religion taught and practiced the doctrine of infant baptism. Using the scriptures, we taught that children should not be baptized until they reach the age of eight years, the age of accountability. (We had also referred to this topic in our first "Message to Israel.")

Following is a portion of the text of our second "Message to Israel":

"Some will ask the question, 'What, if anything, should be done for the children?' The answer is that the children should be blessed. Read Matthew 19:13–15; Mark 10:13–16.

"In these scriptures, Jesus Christ Himself took the little children up into His arms and blessed them. He did not sprinkle them or baptize them. He blessed them.

"It is quite apparent that the disciples of Jesus felt that the children were unworthy to go before the Master, so they rebuked them. To this, Jesus was 'much displeased' (Mark 10:14), and He ordered them to be brought to Him, 'for of such is the kingdom of heaven' (Matthew 19:14). I am sure that He is equally displeased with the infant baptisms and sprinklings of today. This information we learn from a prophet of God named Joseph Smith—the same man who, through heavenly guidance, established the *true* church and the *true* teachings of Jesus Christ." (See Appendix E for the full text.)

Both of our messages to Israel were written in English and Niuean, duplicated, and distributed to anyone who would receive them. For many weeks after we distributed this second message concerning baptism, we taught the subject in detail. Months later, while we were visiting some of the back villages, a few people in the village of Makefu asked if we would remain for a while. This was unusual, because we had not had much success there. But they said they had something they wanted us to do.

Radio (right) and Sam Uati with latest catch.

The Children of Makefu

The villagers' request that we remain for a while led to another great outpouring of the Spirit to these dear, humble people. Having heard our teachings of the doctrine of blessing infants rather than baptizing them, these villagers had become convinced of its truth. To our surprise, joy, and pure delight, several people brought their children to us and asked us in a quiet and gentle way to give them a name and a blessing through the priesthood of God. None of these parents were members of the Church; all of them were afraid of the potential consequences if they were baptized. However, because of the love they had for their children, they overcame some of their fear and brought their children forward for a blessing.

We desired to give these people and their children all we could in order to strengthen them. Through the power of the priesthood, we blessed and named their children one by one. There were 16 of them that day in October 1952, all under the age of eight. I believe it was Radio Safiu Uati who carefully recorded their names, along with their ages and the names of their parents. (See a copy of this list in his original handwriting, appendix F.)

Name	Age	Matua tane (father)	Matua fifine (mother)
Sionesatini	6	Tohovaka	Gasisihetupe
Ikimata	5	Tohovaka	Gasisihetupe
Inagaletiatia	1	Tohovaka	Gasisihetupe
Masiolenau	4	Panikitau	Hegatakai

Makatoni	4	Panikitau	Hegatakai
Feuahitama	1	Pitasoni	Mamatahemotu
Lene	5	Pitasoni	Mamatahemotu
Malamaheva	6	Konakava	Siolohiva
Fakaosiagatau	3	Konakava	Siolohiva
Mokasitatalama	2	Konakava	Siolohiva
Taulagahau	7	Fakalaga	Lauola
Famani	5	Fakalaga	Lauola
Kalaunitama	4	Kalauni	Ahitogaloa
Maasomele	3	Vikita	Ilatagaloa
Kololino	2	Vikita	Ilatagaloa
Manogiole	1	Fakalaga	Lauola

I feel that the names of these parents should be placed with the names of those 42 noble ones who were first baptized in Niue. Although some of these parents and children were not baptized until a later date, I feel that they must be noted as being among the first to demonstrate their great faith. During the following months, they became helpful to us in many ways. We learned to love them and appreciate their courage.

When my wife and I visited Niue in November 2000, we found Sionesatini, the first child listed above. He is now the chief of police for Niue Island. He is a very strong, confident man—well educated, extremely articulate in both languages, and a potential leader for Niue. Sionesatini freely admits to receiving the Lord's blessing all his life.

Elder Bailey giving candy to his group of young Niuean boys.

About Those Boils

During this time, I was enduring a personal physical problem that caused a great deal of discomfort and was extremely painful at times. Large boils appeared on my skin and almost instantly grew to a size larger than a silver dollar. This problem continued for many months. Sometimes I had as many as 10 to 15 infections at one time. On some occasions I was unable walk or ride my bike to the back villages because of them. The local medical people had no solution except to lance them to relieve the pressure.

My associates at the mission home in Auckland said I was enduring the plagues of Job. In his letter to me written on 28 July 1952, President Ottley wrote: "I hope you are rid of your boils. They say that they are purifiers. I don't know anything else that would recommend them to the good of man." However, the boils would continue on for some time.

Six

NEW MOMENTUM

AFTER THE BAPTISMS of our first 42 faithful Saints in the Amanau Cave and the blessing of the 16 children in Makefu, the work in Niue took on new momentum. We thought it was time to redecorate our meeting place, the Blue Bell.

A New Look for the Old Blue Bell

As mentioned earlier, the Blue Bell building consisted of a concrete slab approximately 30 feet by 30 feet, with roof and sides of rusting corrugated tin. There were no windows or doors, just openings. There was no furniture, only palm woven mats.

Our first effort was to paint the rusty roof. Our dear, eager young men did this in short order. The only paint they could find was a brown-red color.

Finding paint for the rest of the building was a little harder. All we could find on the whole island, in any color, was one gallon of aluminum paint that we could buy from the government. At the time, most of the local buildings had thatched roofs and lime-plastered walls and required very little maintenance. There was not much need for paint stores on the island.

We started painting with that one gallon of aluminum paint and kept pouring in kerosene as an additive until we finished the entire exterior. We are not sure how we painted the whole building with just one gallon, but we did. (Maybe it was because the British gallon is bigger than the American gallon. But that much bigger? Probably not.) We called that paint bucket our little miracle. We were certainly violating the laws of physics.

The Old Blue Bell with a new face—the main meeting place for the Church in Niue.

After that back-bending painting job, we walked a few feet away from the building to admire our labors. It looked just beautiful. Regardless of its unorthodox history and the austerity of its non-religious design, the old Blue Bell—now silver—looked beautiful to us. We were so pleased and grateful to have our own place of worship, no matter how humble.

Our Method of Proselyting

From the beginning of our missionary labors on Niue Island, our approach in doing missionary work was always to begin by expressing our love and concern for the individual and the family. As we would meet them at their level and share the truth with them, many people would develop confidence in us. When they knew we really cared, they began to trust us and listen to our message. We would sit with them on the ground, on the mats, or in their huts. They would share their food with us, and we would share ours with them. We would laugh and cry with them. We would pray with them and share their victories or sorrows.

Then we introduced them to new ideas, new skills, and new ways of doing things. We began with songs, both new and familiar, theirs and ours. We shared new games, such as volleyball and baseball, and new activities, such as square dancing. We later introduced boxing, which was very popular in New Zealand.

Elder Goodman with Miriama, Pape, and family.

Then, in this setting, we shared the priceless gift of the knowledge of God and of His glorious work of the Restoration among the children of men in these last days. Many people received our message with great joy and happiness as it was attested to by the Spirit.

Taking the Gospel to New Villages

Whenever we went to a new village to present the gospel, particularly if we knew no one who lived there, our procedure was as follows:

We would always take some of our young Niuean members with us to help us get acquainted and to help interpret our message. We would usually enter a village in the early evening because most of the people would

Preparing for fiafia, 1952.

be at work in their plantations during the day. After locating ourselves in the center of the village, we would place a woven mat on the ground, lay our books and kerosene lantern on the mat, and sit down. We needed a lantern because most of our meetings would continue past sundown.

Then one of us would stand up and begin singing a hymn, and we would all join in. Then we would have a prayer. By then some people would start to gather—children first, and then some of the older villagers. All sat upon the ground to listen to our message. People were usually very courteous and listened attentively, but there were very few or no responses or questions. At the conclusion we would usually greet the people individually, express our appreciation, and leave.

Elder DeWitt at our new home at Utuko, Alofi, 1952.

A New Home for the Missionaries

Another small miracle happened at about this time. It is very rare that island traders (local merchants) would leave the island. Their tenures were usually 20 to 25 years long. However, for some reason, Mr. and Mrs. H. T. Duane, owners of a trading establishment, decided to leave. Their house at Utuko in Alofi became available.

Considering the deficiencies of Anakale, our "cave of the birds" (which Elder Christensen bluntly labeled in his journal as "a dump"), we felt that almost anything would be an improvement. The house at Utuko would be a dream come true. We acted quickly and soon arrived at an agreement. Arrangements were made that we would occupy the house on 11 October 1952, the day after the Duanes were scheduled to leave on the *Tofua*.

There wasn't much furniture. After making negotiations with Captain Bell, we borrowed some small pieces of furniture from Anakale. Since the Duanes were taking their refrigerator with them, we still would not have one of those remarkable appliances. In fact, we wouldn't have one for 13 additional months, when mission headquarters would finally send us a small kerosene refrigerator from Auckland.

Elder Christensen made this comment in his journal concerning our move from Anakale to Utuko: "Today we moved into our new house. It is really going to be nice. It is just like moving from a tent into a mansion. We have Mariama and Wilson [Moumou] to do our cooking. Our box of kai [food] came from NZ so at last we have some decent *kai* to eat. We really feel happy and it has lifted our morale up about 100%" (ECJ, 331).

Papi, left, later became our cook at Utuko.

More Problems with Boils

During this time my "Job-like" plague of boils continued giving me serious problems, temporarily slowing us down. Elder Christensen record-ed: "Elder Goodman has been very sick today. He has a cold in his chest, boils all over his left leg, and big blisters on his feet. He is really sick. I am now holding a 24-hour fast for him. The old Devil is doing all in his power to stop us from doing this work" (ECJ, 306–7).

Elder Basil DeWitt Arrives

The *Tofua* that arrived on 10 October 1952 brought another great blessing to Niue in the person of Elder Basil E. DeWitt. Elder DeWitt was indeed one of God's special servants. When called to serve in the New Zealand mission, he was about 65 years old. At full stature, he stood about five feet tall. Full of life and love for everyone he met, he had an engaging personality that soon put all strangers at ease. He loved the Church and did all he could to promote the work.

Elder DeWitt with new canoes.

Besides his wonderful grandfatherly spirit and attitude, he was an accomplished artist. He saw beauty in just about everything. He would spend most of his time telling stories and painting beautiful landscape scenes on coconut hulls, faces of watches, canvas, pillow cases, walls, or just about anything one might desire. He preached the gospel of love to everyone, no matter who or what they were. All the natives of Niue who knew Elder DeWitt loved him. Children sought him continually. Even the white *papalagi* (Europeans) liked him and sought his company. He was a bright star and a refreshing breeze to us all.

Elder DeWitt was on Niue for only 94 days—just long enough to help strengthen our work and allow me to leave the island at one point for a 20-day respite with President Ottley. But what a great 94 days those were! Speaking for both of us, Elder Christensen wrote: "Elder DeWitt is sure a

Elder Basil DeWitt arrives in Niue, October 1952.

64

Elder DeWitt and children at Utuko.

wonderful little man. I sure do love him and I know that everyone does who knows him" (ECJ, 333). "He has a very good method of proselyting by means of his wonderful paintings" (ECJ, 341). "People come around home to have a look at Elder DeWitt's paintings. His painting is a marvelous means of proselyting the gospel" (ECJ, 334).

"We had a little fun with Elder DeWitt today," continued Elder Christensen. "He was teasing us so we filled up the [bath] tub and put him in it, clothes and all. He is really a good sport. He took it in good fashion. We certainly have a good time with him around. We had MIA this evening. Elder DeWitt held another art show. [The next day,] Elder DeWitt and I finished painting the Blue Bell [inside] as much as we are going to. Looks pretty good. I had Elder DeWitt cut my hair today and I will be darned if he didn't cut it all off. I was really surprised, but I guess he was just getting even with me" (ECJ, 340).

Resident Commissioner Larsen, a Good Friend

Some of our great pleasures, and a little diversity from our usual work, were the occasions when we spent time with Resident Commissioner Larsen and his family. They had a young son who lived with them. Their two daughters were at school in New Zealand. In his mid-to-late 40s, Mr. Larsen was a big man physically and was in great health and vigor. He loved life and enjoyed almost everyone with whom he came in contact. He had a warm smile and a quick wit. He loved the people of Niue and was dedicated to their progress.

Niue's Resident Commissioner, Cecil Hector Watson Larsen with family, 1952

As the island's resident commissioner, he also served as the judge of the high court of Niue. Some say he was a strict disciplinarian.

There was a small golf course (filled with coral rock) that had been built on the island by the government. Mr. Larsen invited us to enjoy many recreational hours together on that little golf course, such as it was. He came by our house often to see how we were doing. And he invited us almost every week to his house. He was certainly a good friend to us and to the Church.

Elder Christensen recorded the following about some of the times we spent with Mr. Larsen: "10/4/52: Mr. Larsen invited us over to his place for the evening. We played Mah-Jongg, a Chinese game. It was very interesting. Had a good conversation of the things pertaining to Niue Island. Had a nice social evening" (ECJ, 327). "Went over to the Larsens and spent the evening. Got home at 12 A.M. Mr. Larsen took us to see his new house and around the farm" (ECJ, 334). "Mr. Larsen can surely do the hula. He is really fun to watch" (ECJ, 327).

President Ottley and a General Authority Visit Niue

The November island run of the *S.S. Tofua* was replaced by a sister ship, the *S.S. Matua*, a small freighter about the size of the *Tofua*. The *Matua* arrived on 7 November 1952, bringing us the usual excitement of contact with the outside world.

That day, however, was a special day. President Ottley arrived with two visitors from Salt Lake City, who had been touring the New Zealand Mission: Bishop Carl W. Buehner, a member of the Presiding Bishopric, and Brother Edward O. Anderson, Church architect. We were delighted and pleased to see these dear brethren. They brought encouragement and inspiration to our humble efforts.

Elder Christensen elaborated on their visit: "November 7th, 1952 – The Matua arrived about 10 A.M. Elder DeWitt, Elder Goodman and I were down on the wharf to greet President Ottley, Bishop Buehner, and Brother Anderson. It was wonderful to see them. They had a good trip. I believe President Ottley has put on a little weight since I saw him three months ago. The first thing we did was take them home to see our living quarters. They were very well pleased with it. Then we showed them the school, Mr. Larsen's new home, the public works, a couple of building lots, and then went down to the Blue Bell for a *fiafia*. They gave us a big *kai* [food] and some beautiful dancing. Bishop Buehner and Brother Anderson had never seen any thing like it before. Each one of the brethren spoke to us all and we certainly did enjoy it. They told the people if they are faithful and prayerful we would soon have us some fine new chapels.

"After the *fiafia* in Alofi we got on a truck and went to Liku and Lakepa where the people put on some more beautiful dances for us. We arrived back home about 7 P.M. dusty and dirty. We cleaned up and went

Miriama, Kouhemotu, and wife, Ataline, preparing to leave for New Zealand.

to Mr. Larsen's home for a couple of hours. We discussed the problems and necessities that we need here in Niue. After leaving Mr. Larsen's home we went on board the ship for two hours or so. President Ottley talked to us and gave us counsel and advice. We all had a lovely day. I couldn't ever ask for a finer day than we had today.

"We said goodbye to them all. Elder Goodman . . . is going away for 20 days or so. Elder DeWitt and I got on a lighter [small boat] and came ashore. We got home about 2 A.M. We have really had a full day of it, but one that I will always remember" (ECJ, 345).

While President Ottley, Bishop Buehner, and Brother Anderson were in Niue, we showed them a piece of land in Alofi that we had been negotiating to lease as a place for a new chapel. They thought the site was good. The lease was finalized. The chapel in Alofi was built on that site, along with the new mission home. (See the original plat of land, Appendix G.)

A Short Respite in Suva, Fiji

President Ottley thought it best that I leave the island for a short period and find a solution to my persistent skin boils. I guess he also thought I needed a short break from the rigors of Niue. Brother Anderson and I stopped at Suva, Fiji, and spent a few days together there while President Ottley and Bishop Buehner continued their journey on the *Matua*. Brother Anderson and I went fishing—something he loved to do—in a rented rowboat in Suva Harbor. We didn't catch much but got plenty of rowing exercise.

Brother Anderson was delightful to be with. Though somewhat reserved according to our youthful standard, he was clever and witty. He was highly intelligent and knew well his craft as a master builder.

At that time, Brother Anderson was just finishing his work on the architectural plans for the Los Angeles Temple, and he showed me some of the plans during our visit. Shirley and I later became one of the first couples married in that temple—on 17 August 1956, shortly after its completion.

A Cure for the Boils—and a Radio

While in Suva I was successful in finding a salve that, if applied early to my infections, would prevent the boils from festering. This was to be the final answer to my problem with boils, but it would be many months before they would all finally go away.

I also purchased an overseas radio receiver for use on Niue. With the right antenna, we could now enjoy listening to what was happening in the outside world. Along with our little kerosene refrigerator, this radio would turn out to be one of the little pleasures and diversions from missionary life on Niue Island.

Seven

THE WORK MOVES FORWARD

DURING MY SHORT VISIT to Suva, Fiji, the work on Niue was going full steam ahead with Elder Christensen and Elder DeWitt. Elder Christensen recorded that they continued teaching in the villages of Makefu, Mutulau, Lakepa, and Liku. With missionary humor, he reported that halfway through a meeting at Lakepa, someone threw large rocks at the little meeting place, so much that it "just about rocked us out of the house because it was so loud" (ECJ, 349). Fortunately, no one was hurt.

Introducing Square Dancing

In Liku, after the regular meeting was over, Elder Christensen introduced good old Utah pioneer-type square dancing as an MIA activity. The people loved it and readily joined in. The meeting had started with about 45 people, but by the time they got to the square dancing part, 75 to 80 people were participating. The dancing lasted about two hours until someone again rained down stones and everyone scattered. This ended the dance, but the people began to love and enjoy that activity.

On 28 November 1952, I returned from Suva, Fiji, to Niue on the *Tofua*. It was a joy to be back on the Rock, such as it was, and to be with my dear brethren and our fellow Saints again.

The Joseph Jackson Family

On 13 November 1952, a couple of weeks before I returned from Suva, Elder Christensen and Elder DeWitt had started teaching the Joseph Jackson family of Alofi, and we held many wonderfully spiritual meetings thereafter. After a few more sessions, however, Brother Joseph told us that the teaching must stop because he had received threats from the LMS

71

Joseph Jackson of Alofi.

church. One of the Jacksons' children had died and was buried in the the LMS church's cemetery. The threat was that if the family continued to listen to the Mormon elders, Brother Joseph would have to exhume his dead child's body and bury it somewhere else. He was further threatened by the demand that his building, which was built a few feet over his property line, would have to be moved.

We stopped teaching the Jackson family, and he and his wife never joined the Church. However, his family did join later, and to this day they are some of the great stalwarts of the Church on Niue. We developed a great love for this wonderful family.

Pews for the Blue Bell

As our little congregation in Alofi began to grow and our meetings became more numerous, we decided we needed to make some more

New benches, tables & rostrum for the Blue Bell.

refinements to the good old Blue Bell. We needed some pews, a sacrament table, a stand, and a rostrum. Not having any sources available and yet having a wonderful creative resource in Elder DeWitt, we decided to do something.

Elder Christensen recorded: "December 6, 1952 – Got up before 6 A.M. this morning and went out to the bush with about 12 of our brethren. We spent all day cutting logs so we can get some wood to make seats for the Blue Bell" (ECJ, 360).

Using axes and two-man crosscut saws, we were able to get enough logs for our project. We took them to the government's saw mill and had the logs cut into rough boards. From these we were able to make 18 benches, a rostrum, a stand, and a sacrament table. To make it all look extra nice, under Elder DeWitt's direction we hand-planed, painted, and grained all the wood.

How beautiful it looked! Our members were delighted to have somewhat of a more formal atmosphere for worship services. The whole project took about five very long weeks to complete. We were working intensely, hoping to get it done before Elder DeWitt had to leave on the January 14th boat. We just barely made it.

Christmas with Our Friends

Christmas of 1952 was extra special for all the Niuean Saints and the three missionaries. It was unlike any Christmas any of us had ever experienced before. We taught the members about our Heavenly Father's wondrous gift to us of His Only Begotten Son. We taught them about the glorious gift of salvation and the Atonement from the Savior Jesus Christ. Then we began to show them how and why we celebrate the birth of Jesus Christ—and how and why we give gifts to others. God's pure love for us, together with His desire that we return to Him, were the motivation for His great gifts to us. This, then, was our reason for giving gifts to each other.

It was so delightful to see our dear Niuean brothers and sisters give gifts to each other at this season, even though they had very little to give. We witnessed again how loving and generous they were. We saw children giving each other a taro or a coconut or a handwoven basket—sweet, humble gifts of what they had. In doing so, they were expressing their love for each other and emulating the love the Father and His Son have for us.

For weeks we elders planned a real American-style Christmas party. From the local trader, we bought balloons, crepe paper, and party hats to

Solomona (center) and other members on new benches, Alofi.

create a bright, festive atmosphere. Elder DeWitt made a huge batch of candy and even painted a large Santa Claus. Elder Christensen typed out some Christmas songbooks, and we made copies for everyone. Of course, we had a Christmas tree with decorations of whatever we had. It was beautiful in its superb natural simplicity.

Elder Christensen wrote: "December 24, 1952 – We all went down to the Blue Bell and decorated it up for our party this evening. We certainly had the old Blue Bell fixed up nice. The members put on

First Alofi congregation.

a very good *fiafia*. Native dances, drama, community singing, square dancing, etc. Each of the kids and adults brought gifts for each other. They put them under the tree. It was wonderful to see the way kids gave gifts to each other. We gave each of the people a hat and some of Elder DeWitt's homemade candy. Gifts consisted mostly of taro, sugar cane, and baskets. These people are very poor [as to the things of the world] and cannot afford very much, but they are happy with what they have. Had well over 100 out tonight. We gave our dear people their first Christmas tree and a real Christmas party. Got to bed at 2 A.M." (ECJ, 372).

"December 25, 1952 – Biked out to Mutulau and held a Christmas meeting with the people. This evening we elders opened up a can of beans for supper and hit the sack about 9 P.M." (ECJ, 373).

New Year's Eve and Gifts from Nuhaka

New Year's Eve brought another happy time for our members. New Year's Eve is one of the happiest times of the year for Niueans. They tend to celebrate vigorously, sometimes not in the manner that the Lord would approve. We decided to help them learn to celebrate it in a more appropriate manner.

Just in time for the event, we received four large packages from the wonderful Saints in Nuhaka, New Zealand, where Elder Christensen had previously served. The packages contained gifts from them to the Saints of Niue. So for our New Year's Eve party, we had enough presents to give one to each person. It was another of those special occasions that everyone enjoyed because of the love and generosity of others. We were deeply

Members on their way to other villages for fiafia.

75

appreciative of those generous Saints in Nuhaka. In appreciation, the Niuean Saints later sent a large package of handwoven baskets, fans, mats, and other items to the Nuhaka Saints. They also sent several shipments of Niuean bananas.

More Baptisms at the Amanau Cave

As the new year started, our baptisms continued. On 2 January 1953 we rented a truck and picked up people from Liku, Makefu, Lakepa, and Alofi and proceeded to the Amanau Cave. We baptized 20 more people that day, bringing our total number of members to 86.

After the baptism, we took everyone to our home at Utuko. There we held a sacrament meeting in which we confirmed them members of the Church and gave them each a blessing. Then we administered the sacrament to these new members for the first time. I am sure the Lord is pleased with those who entered the Church that day.

After sacrament meeting, we took the people to their homes and then went on to Liku to hold another Bible study class. We arrived home that night at 10:30 P.M.—tired and hungry, but filled with joy for the happenings of the day.

A New Year's Letter of Greeting from President Ottley

President Ottley sent us the following letter, dated 12 January 1953:

"To the Latter-day Saints and friends at Niue:

"At the beginning of this new year we here all wish you every happiness for 1953 and pray the Lord to bless you with health and strength and all other blessings that will make life pleasant. Especially the blessings of hope and peace in the home and in your villages. That the power of the evil one will not make life hard for you and that your meetings and your parties and your games may all be attended by the Spirit of the Lord Jesus Christ.

"If men speak evil, answer

President Sidney J. Ottley in New Zealand.

them with good; if they persecute you, do good to them; if they teach hate and cursings, teach them the Gospel of love; if they cast you out, invite them to your meetings. Our Lord teaches that a soft answer turneth away wrath but grievous words stir up anger. In patience we will win over the bad spirit that our enemies have shown.

"Elders Goodman and Christensen will be as fathers to you if you give them your faith and your confidence. They will guide you in the path of right for they are men of God and bear the holy priesthood which blesses men and does not curse them. They will teach you the true gospel of the Savior and will not tell false tales about you to other people as some of your leaders have done.

"Listen closely to their words and study them and read your Bibles and have them teach you the true gospel as it is so plainly taught. You are a blessed people and are the children of Israel. We will, sooner or later, have a little place of our own to meet in, our numbers will grow, and we will be a very happy and contented people.

"Sincerely your brother,

"Sidney J. Ottley, Mission President"

Ambushed Outside the Village of Toi

At the north end of the island, between the larger villages of Hikutavake and Mutulau, is the smaller village of Toi. On Monday, 5 January 1953, we entered Toi for the first time and started preaching the restored gospel to the villagers there. About 50 people gathered to listen to us. We had an enjoyable meeting and thought we had made a few friends.

But a few days later, when we made our next visit to Toi, something unusual happened. We went to the center of the village and put our woven mat on the ground, as usual, placing our books and kerosene lantern on the mat. We sang our hymn and had a prayer as usual. But to our surprise, no one came. Not one person appeared. We could see children peeking out from behind distant coconut trees, but no one came near. We concluded our message, gathered up our materials, and left.

After traveling several hundred yards through the thick bush back toward the village of Alofi, we encountered a barricade of cut tree branches about three or four feet high across the narrow road. Then we heard loud noises and screams behind us and all around us. A group of people quickly made a second barricade on the path behind us. We were trapped between the two barricades. Then, as the yelling continued, people started setting fire to the bush that completely surrounded us.

We watched as the fire grew higher and higher. But no one in our group panicked. Instead, we remained calm as we remembered our prayers of that morning and throughout the day. We felt that the attack

Road through bush to Alofi.

on us had been inspired by Satan, but we truly had no fear because we knew the Lord was with us and would protect us. Rather than feeling afraid, we were simply curious about what these dear children of God had in mind for us.

After a while, the blazing barricade on the trail leading to Alofi burned down somewhat, reducing in size sufficiently to allow us to quickly step over the fire and proceed on our way home.

Our Return to Toi

We returned to Toi several days later, on 19 January 1953. Without any mention of what had happened during our previous visit, we went on with our usual meetings. This time the atmosphere was very different. Nearly everyone in the village attended and listened very carefully to our message.

As time went on, everyone—as far as we know—in the village of Toi was baptized and became members of the Church. So great was their faith that, without prompting from us, they built their own small thatched meeting place where we could come and teach them. It was a lovely, though humble, little place of about 12 feet by 15 feet in size. To me, it became a monument to their faith. Though not officially dedicated by a priesthood holder, it was a sacred place to us all. We loved going there. We loved being with those dear people of Toi.

Today there is a beautiful chapel built by the church in Toi, one of

People in the village of Toi.

the five on the island of Niue. It stands as a monument to those faithful members who tested us, received our message, and endured the persecution of many of their native countrymen. They remained steadfast in the faith. Indeed, they need to be counted with those faithful few who stood their ground and trusted in the Lord. Today they are a blessed people.

255 Meetings in 180 Days

Teaching continued as usual, with varying degrees of success. Despite setbacks, we were pleased and delighted with our progress. The Lord was surely blessing and providing for us. At one point, Elder Christensen recorded that since the day he had arrived on Niue, 180 days earlier, we had held approximately 255 meetings and had biked more than 65 miles per week (see ECJ, 397, 404). I guess he should know; he was indeed a faithful record keeper.

Hit—but Not Hurt Badly

On the evening of 28 January 1953, we biked out to Lakepa and had one of our usual meetings with friends and investigators. They seemed happy and enjoyed the meeting. But as we left the village and started pedaling home, we were peppered again with stones.

This time Elder Christensen suffered some injury. One stone skimmed along the side of his head; it parted his hair but did no real damage to his head. But another stone struck him solid on the side of his foot; that injury was very painful and lasted several days. He soon recovered and later recorded, "Oh well, it's not every missionary that gets rocks thrown at them" (ECJ, 394).

With the exception of Elder Barrett (who was driven with me into the bush one night and ended up having to leave Niue prematurely because he injured his feet on poisonous coral), this was the only time any of us was ever hurt by the stonings, even though we were targeted 20 to 30 times during those early days. I was never hit by stones—probably because I was too skinny to be a significant target.

However, as I have mentioned, boils were very painful and debilitating at times. Elder Christensen had problems with a facial cyst and with stiffness in his neck that lasted for some time. We were sincerely grateful for the divine protection and significant lessons learned by these difficulties.

On our next visit to Lakepa, we had an even larger crowd of people. We had a very good meeting, and most of the people seemed interested. As we left the village, one of the older men walked with us a little way down the road to make sure no more rocks would be thrown.

A Brief Moment of Discouragement

Sometimes in the life of a missionary, there can be a few brief moments of discouragement, particularly for missionaries so far from home, as we were, and who had been serving under our current circumstances for nearly two years.

One of those moments occurred on 9 February 1953, just 11 days after the stoning incident mentioned above. Elder Christensen, man of steel and velvet, wrote in his journal: "Just another day in the life of *Ko* (me) Christensen. Nothing ever happens exciting around this place. It's as dead as can be some days. Oh well" (ECJ, 398). Little did he or I know about the things that were about to happen over the next six months.

Baptizing Moumou

A few days later, on the evening of 17 February 1953, another of those wonderfully touching events happened. We took Wilson "Moumou" MacMoore to Amanau Cave and baptized him. Remember

Moumou? He was the young man who became my temporary companion after Elder Barrett's untimely departure from Niue. He remained a good and faithful companion until Elder Christensen arrived. Even though he had not been baptized, he had worked with us diligently through all our hardships. But for some reason, he was had not been quite ready to be baptized until now.

Moumou and friend on Niue shoreline.

His baptism was a very special event for us all. Elder Christensen observed: "There were just the three of us. It was a beautiful sight. I will never forget the wonderful feeling that comes over me when we take these people down to that cave where there we baptize them members of God's true church that has been restored for his children here in the last days" (ECJ, 403).

Eight
STORIES OF FAITH

THERE ARE MANY wonderful faith-promoting stories of events occurring in the lives of these early Saints of Niue. Great and pure indeed was their faith in God. They lived close to nature and relied upon it for every aspect of their lives. And the God of nature, whatever their concept of Him was, was always in the hearts of most of them. When we began to teach of the Restoration of the gospel, of prophets, and of the true personality of God, many became intensely interested. When we established these truths with Bible scriptures, their hearts were filled with love and appreciation for God and for us as His humble servants who brought them the message.

Although I am reluctant to relate stories of the Niueans' faith for fear of leaving someone out, I must share at least three such examples to represent the many.

Rangi, the "Queen of Niue"

Her real name is Lagitafuke Viliko Fakahoa, OBE, but we all call her Rangi, the "queen of Niue." I would surely place her at the top of the list of those first Niueans to receive a testimony of the restored gospel. Rangi was a Samoan by birth. She was well educated and extremely intelligent. She understood English as well as Samoan. Brother Fritz Krueger, himself a Samoan, taught her the gospel in the Samoan and English languages, and she received and understood the message very quickly. The Spirit bore witness to her of the truthfulness of the work, and she soon developed a wonderful, strong testimony of the true gospel of Jesus Christ.

Brother Solomona and one of his big fish.

It is interesting to note that the first Niuean Christian, Peniamina—for whom there is a special recognition day each year in Niue—received his knowledge and testimony of Jesus Christ in Samoa. He was the first to spread Christianity in Niue (1845), to be helped later by Paulo, another Samoan missionary (1849). Then, more than 100 years later, one Samoan, Brother Fritz Krueger, shared the restored gospel with another Samoan/Niuean, Sister Rangi, when the restored gospel was first introduced to Niue Island. The Lord indeed must love the Samoan and Niuean people to give so much to them and expect so much from them.

With a burning testimony born of the Spirit, Rangi became unrelenting in assisting us in establishing the Church in Niue. She possessed faith greater than we could comprehend. For this, and her unconquerable spirit, we learned to love and cherish her. The Spirit of the Lord was surely with her. Whenever there were meetings to be held, lessons to be taught, or people to be loved and encouraged, Rangi was there.

Rangi was our first bridge over the language and cultural barriers of Niue. It would have been next to impossible for us to have proceeded to build up the Church in those days without Rangi and others like her. We knew in our hearts that the Lord had called her and placed her there.

The personal sacrifices and privations Rangi and her family endured were many. Following is her own account of some highlights of her life, as told to Ikimautama Ikimau at Rangi's residence in Auckland, New Zealand, on 14 February 2002. Giving her story the title "My Right Stride Forward," Rangi begins with a history of her experiences in the Church and concludes with her personal history:

"My folks were staunch members and followers of the London Missionary Society religion. They first affiliated with them when we were living in Western Samoa, and they continued on when we came to Niue. My dad was a firm believer of its principles and held a position of a leading deacon. This gave me no choice but to be with my parents and assist them in their doings. At that time, that was the only religion to rely on in the entire island—and had been since Niue's early history. In all respect, we need to give them credit for introducing the word of the Lord and the Bible to the people of Niue, even though some of its principles were somewhat debatable.

"The Mormon Church, as it was commonly known among the Niue people at that time, was introduced to the island by Brother Krueger and his family. Because Fritz Krueger was, himself, a Samoan, that obviously made our acquaintance easier. Listening to the Mormon teachings and its gospel principles brought home to me how poor my knowledge of things pertaining to God and the purposes for which we were created really were.

"I embraced these teachings, and I knew within myself that they were true. I wanted to be baptized. However, my respect for my dad's position in his church and his responsibility as a village constable hampered my enthusiasm. After I discussed the matter with my dad, he gave his blessing with a firm assurance that I should proceed to do what I knew was best for me. With that assurance in place, I accepted the challenge from the elders to be baptized and become a member of The Church of Jesus Christ of Latter-day Saints.

"In the evening of August 14th, 1952, I was among the 26 souls who marched single file down the cliff to the Amanau Cave. There, by lamplight, the first baptisms in Niue Island were performed under the authority of the holy priesthood by Elder Goodman, Elder Christensen, and Brother Krueger.

"Accepting these lifesaving ordinances was not without challenges. The adversary, through the opposition, was raging. We heard vile, insulting words, but we were not hurt. Physical harm was threatened but not carried out.

"Although we were few in number, we were one and united. We bonded as a unified body in our faith and trust in God as we rejoiced in our new-found knowledge of Him and our relationship with Him. Because of this we were enabled to overcome whatever the opposition would throw at us. It was this oneness of spiritual strength in the pioneer days of the Church in Niue that we were able to boldly uphold the truthfulness of the gospel with our might and our strength.

"I accepted callings to serve in the branch, from Relief Society to Primary leadership positions, in the infant days of the Church. Since there was only a handful of us, we toiled together as a united body. For example, we were required to raise 20 percent of the total cost for our new chapel to be built. Money was not easy to find. Most of our members were not engaged in paid employment. But with our human qualities of perseverance, sacrifice, hard work, dedication, and teamwork in a true Mormon spirit, we managed to secure our 20 percent. It came through our "bring-and-buy" system and by manpower. We labored by hauling rocks to the rock crusher and crushing it for the chapel and for the foundation of the new mission home. We also carried water from the seashore and from the Burn-Philips Store water tank for mixing concrete. We toiled by hand to meet all the challenges requested by our priesthood leaders—from feeding the missionaries and mending their clothes to other manual labor. These were some of the significant manual works completed by a few people with the spirit of oneness and for one purpose.

"Oh, how wonderful it was just wonderful to associate with my fellow sisters in the gospel! To my dear Sisters Miliama Vatu, Papi Tanevesi, Fay Uati, Foini Hekau, Mahine Solomona, Fineone Heka, Vesitama Asekona, Tifahega Ikimau, Nuasa Olife, and Kolikoli Makahu, I give my undying love and sincere appreciation for their help and service to the Lord.

"And to my own dear mother, Tuiolo Haioti, and to my other sisters in the gospel and their children in the village of Avatele, the village of Mutulau, the village of Lakepa, the village of Tuapa, the village of Liku, and the village of Toi, I express my love and appreciation.

"Our numbers were few, but as we accomplished great things through our self-sacrifice and hard work, we demonstrated to our fellow Niuean friends the truthfulness of the Mormon Church. I would say with all integrity that we have left behind a marvelous legacy, and we have built a solid foundation of the Church in Niue. Those who will come after us can enjoy it with no fear of intimidation from any other people. There is hope. There is joy waiting for all of us.

"One of the joys of my membership was when my husband and I were called to the land of our birth [Samoa] to serve as a proselyting missionary couple. We were enthusiastic with our calling. We were prepared to give our all to meet our responsibilities. We walked the villages and visited the people in their humble abodes. We bore to them our testimonies of the truthfulness of the Mormon Church. We enlightened them with the knowledge of the Book of Mormon. The people responded positively to our approaches. Our teaching list was long, and expectations of good reward were high.

"Unfortunately, in the calmness of the early hours of one evening, my missionary companion, my dear beloved husband, was involved in a motor vehicle accident. He died instantly. I returned to Auckland with the remains of my sweetheart, my missionary companion. There he was buried and ended his mortal missionary calling. For me, my missionary duty did not end with the death of my companion. A new companion was called for me. I express my sincere thank-you to Sister Mamili Togiatomai, who was specially called to be my companion for the last eight months of our—my husband's and my—missionary duties here in Auckland.

"It was not expected that we end the mission of our life in this way.

I have no animosity toward the young man who controlled the vehicle that killed my husband, the father of our children, my loved one, my eternal companion. I miss you, my dear husband, very, very much. Every time I think of you, it brings tears to my eyes. I love you. The teachings of the Church we both loved gave great help to me in my hours of loneliness."

Rangi also shared more of her personal history: "I was blessed to be a daughter to a good father and a good mother. So also my two brothers and a sister. I was born on 17 August 1922, in the village of Malifa Apia, Western Samoa. When I was age 13, we left Samoa for Niue Island. This indeed gave me a treasured knowledge of my two separate heritages, Samoan and Niuean. Although I lived in Niue practically all my life, I still managed to speak both languages fluently.

"I attended Niue Island public school, resided at Tufukia, Alofi South. Since it was a school sponsored by New Zealand, it used New Zealand education methods. It was limited, however; the highest class was form 2.

"After graduation there, I secured a position as a teacher. I taught primary-aged pupils. During my time there as a teacher, I was sent twice to New Zealand to further my teaching skills. The teaching lessons I obtained from these year-long observation courses methodically assisted me with my work in helping my pupils learn better. Today the Niue Island education courses of study are level with the New Zealand education system.

"During my time when I was employed as a teacher, I had reasons for concern. Even though the leader of our department was none other than my very own auntie, quite often my name was left off the list of those recommended for promotion. Promotion meant a rank advancement and pay increase. Indeed, it was disheartening. However, I personally considered this as a challenge and an incentive to me. I was determined to promote myself through my performance. I toiled long and hard to lift my performance above that of the other fellow teachers without putting anyone down. In the end my efforts were rewarded twofold.

"The class I taught was selected as an observing class for any school officials visiting our school. Because of my consistent good performance, the school principal assigned me to manage higher responsibilities within the school. I embarked on these responsibilities with vigor to the end of my service with the Niue Island education department.

"After 36 years of service I retired, as was required by the education department statutes. I left behind a profession that was so dear to my heart. I also left behind the little children I had come to love and adore.

"After my retirement my husband, Viliko Maliko Fakahoa, and I decided to leave behind everything and migrate to New Zealand. The decision was not an easy one; however, the future well being of our children was paramount in our deliberations. We were blessed with a daughter, Olove Tauveve Fakahoa (now married to Patrick Novalu Jacobsen) and two sons, Organ Viliko Fakahoa and John Viliko Fakahoa.

"While in New Zealand I searched for an opportunity to involve myself with the concept of education for the under-school-age children of Pacific Islands origins. After I had done much door knocking and talking to anyone who would listen, our reasoning finally reached the people with authority over that age-group of children.

"A Pacific Islands Preschool course was established as a trial. It proved a success. The efforts were rewarded twofold. First, the school's governing body recognized it, and second, the government began funding its operation. Now the Pacific Island Nations Preschool courses here in New Zealand are blossoming and are scattered all over the country.

"Unexpected, yet most humbly appreciated, the New Zealand government approved a recommendation that I receive a royal recognition for my service to the community, and in particular, for my service to teaching. The recognition was made and an award extended. The award was an OBE (Order of the British Empire). My name is now followed with a title. It is Lagitafuke Viliko Fakahoa OBE."

Sister Rangi, continuing with her wonderful intellectual talents, translated 65 Church hymns into Niuean and also started with a group to translate portions of the Book of Mormon.

Rangi, this wonderful sister whose name now bears a title from royalty, will always be in our hearts. She is an inspiration to us all. I will always think of her as the "queen of Niue." At this writing, she still lives in her large, beautiful home in Auckland, New Zealand, with her children and grandchildren, whom she gathers often around her with supreme love as a hen would gather her chickens.

Solomona Ukamotu and the Fish

Brother Solomona Ukamotu was among our first 42 baptized. He was the first Niuean to receive the Aaronic Priesthood.

Brother Solomona was one of the really great ones who helped tirelessly with the Lord's work from the beginning. He was well educated and extremely intelligent. I believe the Lord gave him a special spiritual calling to help us with the work, as the Lord did for so many others at that time. He spoke and wrote Niuean and English fluently. He was employed as secretary to Police Chief Anderson and served as translator for the government. He was a little older than most of the other young men, about 28 years old. He was a dear brother whom we will always love and appreciate.

On 19 March 1953, at about 11:30 P.M., as we returned from one of our long, hard trips to Lakepa and were preparing to retire, Brother Solomona appeared at our door. His whole being appeared totally spent and completely exhausted. His usual strong, confident countenance had fallen and turned to one of deep humility. He looked like one who had just stared the end of mortality in the face and lived to tell of it, one who had just walked that fine line between life and a terrible death and had survived.

He was wet, scared, bruised, and in such a state of trauma that he trembled and cried uncontrollably. It took him a little while before he could speak. As we sat him down and reached out to comfort him, he told us the following story.

Brother Solomona said he had just about lost his life at sea that night. While fishing in the open ocean, he snagged a large *vahekura* (yellow-fin tuna)fish. The fish was so large that it took a long, hard struggle to get it close enough to his canoe to stab it with his knife. After what seemed like hours of total physical exertion, he was able to get the fish within striking range. He struck once with his knife. The fish responded with a terrific sweep of its powerful tail and cracked a hole in his outrigger canoe. The water started gushing in. Solomona quickly tied the end of the fishing line to the canoe and dived into the water. By this time the fish had taken the 200 feet of line, along with the canoe, and had headed out to sea. Solomona yelled out to another man who was nearby to come and help. The record reflects that the man, who was of the other religion, disregarded Solomona's cry for help and instead went after the fish. This left Solomona alone in the ocean, more than a quarter mile from shore, with no floating devices.

He had been fishing near the place called the "point," where the sea was very rough. As he started to swim toward the shore, three huge successive waves took him under. He said he was praying hard, and each time a wave would take him under, something always gave him strength to make it to the surface again.

Solomona continued to swim with all his remaining strength. Struggling mightily, he finally made it to the reef. The ocean was breaking and pounding the reef with such great intensity that it was causing serious undertow. Each time Solomona attempted to grab the reef, the undertow pulled him down. After praying again and, once more, exerting all his strength, he finally caught hold of the reef and waited for the next large wave to push him over into the small lagoon. A wave came and provided the help.

As soon as he realized he was safe on land, he fell to his knees and thanked God. When he arose, he proceeded up the side of the cliff. Upon reaching the top he again fell to his knees, and in tears he humbly thanked God for preserving him from the depths of the sea. After he arose from that prayer, his first stop was at the home of the elders.

With total humility of his soul, Brother Solomona bore to us this simple yet magnificent testimony. He said God had saved his life. He knew that if he hadn't prayed as he did and hadn't lived God's teachings as he knew them, he never would have made it back alive. He testified with great power that he knew God lived and was there with him. He was grateful for the Restoration of the gospel that we had brought and shared with him.

Brother Solomona wanted us to have a special prayer for him and to again thank the Lord. So we knelt together, gave our thanks to God, and asked a special blessing for this noble son.

We later learned that the other fisherman, who went after the fish instead of helping Brother Solomona,

Brother Solomona and one of his big fish.

was successful in catching and killing it. He then managed to tow it to shore behind his outrigger. It was one of those large *valekura* (yellow-fin tuna)—more than nine feet long and very thick of body. (Its weight was not known.) It was then pulled down the road to Solomona's home. There, I hope, it was shared with everyone.

Four Young Niuean Boys

This story began on the day and at the very hour that the first meeting of The Church of Jesus Christ of Latter-day Saints on Niue Island was being held. Before we full-time missionaries had arrived on the island, Brother and Sister Fritz Krueger and their six young daughters were having their first Sabbath-day meeting on Niue in their home in the village of Alofi. As four young Niuean boys passed by the Krueger home, they heard sweet singing and decided to look into it.

The four boys were Ikimautama Ikimau, Makamau Hekau, Tuimaitoga Fakalu, and his brother Kaue Fakalu. The story continues as written by Ikimau, one of the boys: "Brother Krueger noticed us and invited us to come in and be with them. The four shirtless boys with eager eyes accepted the invitation. After all, in the group were two girls our own age. This (maybe) attracted and interested us more than the singing. 'Shine On' was the hymn. It became a familiar hymn in many of the Church meetings

Tuimaitoga climbs up a coconut tree for young, green coconuts.

afterwards. This was the Krueger family's very first Sunday on Niue. It was also the first Church meeting ever conducted on Niue Island."

We would be most ungrateful not to recognize the hand of the Lord and the whisperings of the Spirit to those four young men that day. They all became valiant and extremely diligent in the Lord's work from that time forward.

Tui and Kaue became our very good friends. They attended most of our meetings and biked the rocky, dusty roads with us missionaries quite often. They would climb the coconut trees to provide nourishment and refreshing drink for us. They acted as translators and companions when we missionaries split up several times a week to cover the many meetings in the back villages.

Tuimaitoga and fresh fish he just caught.

Later, after Tui and Kaue were baptized, they suffered very difficult problems of religious persecution brought on by their older brother, who objected to their joining the Mormon Church. In his rage, he beat them severely. He broke Kaue's arm and left him close to death. He also drove them from their home. Tui cared for his brother and nursed him back to health, but Kaue carried many scars from that beating. Later both boys moved to New Zealand. Both are deceased as of this writing. We will always remember and love Tui and Kaue for their loyalty to the elders.

Ikimautama Ikimau and Makamau Hekau were also baptized. They became strong, dedicated Church leaders—and continue faithful today.

Both Ikimau and Makamau were married and sealed to their families in the temple. Ikimau and his wife moved to New Zealand, where he became the first Niuean to be ordained a high priest and a bishop. He loves the Church and serves in many callings today. He is a noble son of God.

Makamau Hekau also loves the Lord and has served Him in many ways. He is now serving as president of the Alofi Niue District of the Tonga Nuku'Alofa Mission.

Nine

ATTEMPTS TO EXPEL THE CHURCH FROM NIUE

"EXPEL" IS A WORD QUITE FAMILIAR in Mormon history. Webster's Dictionary offers the following definition: "To drive or force out." That is precisely what the other religion had been attempting to do to The Church of Jesus Christ of Latter-day Saints for nearly a year since our arrival on Niue. Now their continuing attempts to drive us off the island began on an entirely different front than the island itself. The new battlefront was the New Zealand Parliament.

Since Niue was a territory of New Zealand, it was governed by the New Zealand Parliament. A petition created by the other church and delivered to the New Zealand government requested that the Mormon Church be completely removed from the island of Niue. The petition was given to Mr. T. Clifton Webb, minister of Island Territories, who did not provide a satisfactory answer. The petitioners then requested that the documents go beyond him and be presented to the New Zealand parliament—which Mr. Webb did.

This action led to several news articles. For example, in early January 1953, an article appeared in the *Auckland Star*, stating that the Mormon missionaries had disturbed the Niueans and needed to be removed. The article quoted a Mr. Craig, foreign secretary of the London Missionary Society, who presented the petition for expulsion. He was quoted as saying that he had been reliably informed that when the Niueans had agreed to come under British rule, the stipulation was made that there should be only one Christian denomination on the island. He also said that the

Stairway down the cliff to the Sea

Mormon missionaries had not made much progress and that their presence disturbed the islanders.

Following are excerpts of a few of the more than 15 letters to the editor that were published in newspapers on this subject. Letters in support of the expulsion came from leaders and sympathizers of the other church. Neutral comments came from several observers. Letters in support of religious tolerance came from many good friends and members of our church, with our own dear President Ottley leading the way. President Ottley later told us that the newspapers had received many more letters, but that wise editors had rejected them because of their extreme content.

Letters from Proponents of Expulsion

Jack Naea, 24 January 1953: "I went to Niue in September 1952 and left again in October. There are two Mormon representatives in Niue. They are trying hard to break the peace. Niue Island has had only one religion from the beginning when Paul and Benjamin (see Peniamina 1846) brought the gospel of God to Niue. I only wish that the government would remove the Mormons from Niue right away. That would save a lot of trouble with the natives."

John Caughley, 27 January 1953: "The Niue people distrust and resent the coming of the Mormon mission. This is confirmed by the very natural, sincere letter of Jack Naea in Saturday's *Star*. I paid an official visit to Niue in 1927. All Niueans are devout Christians. All the Mormons could do is to proselytize some simple, genuine Christians to their own sect, thus introducing schism and dissention within the village family or between village and village. Mormons could better direct their energies to the heathen. In their own interests, the Niue villagers should keep their communities closed to Mormon infiltration, and our government should not in any way facilitate it."

Letters from Neutral Observers

P.J.G., 28 January 1953: "Recent correspondence suggests an urgent need for greater tolerance between the denominations in the mission field. The field is large and the laborers are few. Our own non-church goers and the island people alike look to the Christian community for tolerance and charity. If they cannot find it in our actions they will certainly never be persuaded by our preaching."

Arthur Wright, January 1953: "Surely a monopoly to any religious body, anywhere, could be but a menace, risk and danger, for human nature, church or otherwise, misuses power if given the chance. I was not and am not a Mormon, yet personally advise fair play—an open field and no favour. My association with [the Mormons] has revealed to me that they are honest, true-living, decent, God-fearing men. Now Sir, as a tree is judged by its fruits, I ask, 'Have any of the Pacific's Mormon Missions been a curse, or in any way harmful to the native peoples or anyone else?' I must offer a resounding no."

Letters from Church Members and Friends: "We Shall Continue . . . with the Lion's Boldness"

George Hall, 28 January 1953: "I have been associated with the Mormon elders for more than 60 years. I have seen nothing but good in their deep devotion to duty for the Christ, and decency and proper decorum towards the Maori people. Anything the Mormon elders have to impart should never be denied the good people of Niue. They are free people in a free county and are at liberty to dip into fountains wherever the rod of Moses has struck, to drink therefrom and be filled, freely and without price."

President Sidney J. Ottley, January and February 1953 (a summary of many articles he wrote): "Our elders went into Niue with the full consent of the New Zealand and Niue authorities; we have paid our way, and we go about our business. We have a purpose that is nobody's business except those who see the beauty of it and desire to listen. We accept no responsibility for the contention of any individual or group. . . .

"We accept the admonition of the Master to 'Go into all the world and preach the gospel to all nations, all tongues and all people.' If men choose to flee or howl when none are pursuing or throwing stones at them, then let them do so. As for us, whom some seek to belittle and deprive us of our legal rights to do what we choose to accept as our duty, *we shall continue in our present course with the lion's boldness* as spoken of by the wise man Solomon. . . .

"The elders of the Church are in Niue at their own expense. They are peaceable and law abiding. They are men who teach 'peace on earth and goodwill to all men' in their word and in their lives. We would that our aggressive friends would do as well. Our teaching presumes not only to teach the gospel of the Lord Jesus Christ, but to help people to live it. Ours is a doctrine of free agency, not of coercion or frightening. I would that our aggressors could say the same, in truth."

Free to Stay on Niue

Later news articles indicated that Mr. T. Clifton Webb, minister of Island Territories, did take the petition to the New Zealand Parliament for consideration. However, it was never heard because the petition was not framed according to parliamentary standing orders. It was returned to its framers for revision, after which it was to be referred to a standing committee of the House for review. Apparently the petition was never redrawn. It therefore died at that point.

Later that year, on 10 August 1953, Mr. C. E. H. Quinn, assistant secretary of Island Territories of New Zealand, paid a visit to Niue. His objective, among other things, was to hold a hearing concerning whether or not the Mormon Church should stay on Niue Island. Apparently the other church, which had such a strong hold upon every aspect of life in Niue, was still making efforts to get the Mormon Church ejected from the island. The hearings were co-chaired by Mr. Quinn and Commissioner Larsen. Many of our Niuean Saints were interviewed, including Solomona, Rangi Fakahoa, and Tongitama. There were many others.

Elder Christensen's journal offers the following: "August 10, 1953 – Brother Tongitama went down to Alofi today to attend a meeting called by Mr. Larsen and Mr. Quinn concerning the Mormon Church. They had a very good meeting and Mr. Quinn, who is (Asst.) Secretary to Island

Togiatama of Lakepa, constable and Church leader.

Territories, was very pleased with the Church here on Niue. He assured the brethren [and sisters] that the Church would *not* have to leave Niue" (ECJ, 496).

Elder Thomas E. Slade, the missionary who was soon to come to Niue and replace me as district president, made the following note in a letter to his parents, dated October 1954: "There is what is called a counselor in each of the 12 villages here in Niue, and all together they are called the Island Council. They have meetings about once a month to discuss village and island affairs. In their last meeting, last week, *they tried again to have the 'Mormons' taken off Niue*, but to no avail."

The efforts of the adversary still goes on. We accept those efforts as another testimony of the truthfulness of our work.

Back to Business As Usual

By March 1953 we had baptized more than 100 people, and the work was moving along well. In his letter of 14 March 1953, President Ottley informed us that he had applied for permission to send more missionaries to Niue. Later correspondence indicated that he had received it.

Baptisms were continuing. Elder Christensen recorded: "April 7th, 1953 – Today we held a baptism at a Makefu Cave (Avaiki). We baptized 15 from Alofi, Liku, Toi, and Makefu. We left on a truck at 5 P.M., picked up the people, and got into Makefu at 8 P.M. Held a meeting at Tohovaka's home, then went down to the cave. Brother Star [owner of the Blue Bell] and Sam [his son] were among those baptized along with Sis. [Fioni Tauhikupala] Hekau and her daughter [Etena Lovi Hekau]. Tuimaitoga and Kaue [two of the boys mentioned in chapter eight] were also baptized. After the baptism we returned to Makefu, where we held another meeting and did the confirmations. Arrived in Alofi at 12 P.M. We had a full day. I'm really tired" (ECJ, 431).

More Missionaries for Niue

President Ottley's letter to us, dated 5 May 1953, announced that two more missionaries were on their way to join us at Niue. They had been interviewed in Salt Lake City by Elder Matthew Cowley, who said he thought they would be suitable for island life and would make good missionaries. They were to travel via the *Aorangi*, my old ship, to Suva, Fiji. There they would board the *Tofua* bound for Niue.

President Ottley indicated that his plan was to meet them on 9 June in Suva and then join them on their trip to Niue. He estimated their arrival in Niue to be 19 June. He also said that due to shortness of time, we would have to train these new young elders in the ways we carried out missionary work in Niue. He cautioned us that we should give " the pleasant side of the story as they are young [both 21] and will need a bit of encouragement, never having any missionary experience before taking on the island. Perhaps that will be an advantage."

Of course, we were excited to receive the news. Elder Thomas E. Slade and Elder Harold L. Bailey were both from Salt Lake City, Utah. During the next six weeks we prepared for their coming.

The New Elders Arrive

On 19 June 1953, the *Tofua* brought Elder Slade and Elder Bailey to Niue Island. President Ottley was with them. It was a wonderful, joyful day to see the work now receiving new blood and gaining strength. Both of these elders were excited at finally arriving after such a long journey. They were fine young men, filled with the spirit of their calling, and they were eager to get started on the challenges that they knew were ahead.

Elder Christensen wrote the following entry in his journal: "June 19th 1053 – *Koe Aho Falaili*. (Today is Friday.) It was a very rainy day all day long. It made things most miserable. The *Tofua* arrived about 8 o'clock. President Ottley, Elder Bailey, and Elder Slade were on it. We had a good time with President Ottley while he was here. We had a *fiafia* at the Blue Bell, after which we took care of all the business. We also really had a nice visit with the new elders. Elder Goodman and I went out to the ship for a private meeting with Pres. Ottley. I was advised that I would be leaving Niue on the 10th of September and would go to Suva, Fiji. I would fly home from there. I guess I won't be seeing the president again until we get back to Zion. Had a most enjoyable day. Our new elders seem to be very nice fellows. The *Tofua* left early today" (ECJ, 468).

The new elders quickly got into the routine of things, as we had been planning for several weeks. They soon became friends and teachers of our ever-growing flock. They loved the work and the people and gave all their strength and energy to help improve the lives of our members. We were now beginning to create little branches in many of the back villages.

The people soon grew to love these fine young servants of God. Since we shared a love of God our Father and His Son Jesus Christ and a sincere love and devotion to truth and to each other, many wonderful things could—and did—begin to happen.

Geologist Looking for Fresh Water

At about this time, the New Zealand government, realizing the need for a fresh-water source and system for Niue Island, sent a geologist to examine the potential. His name was Mr. Jim Shoefield. Because we had been in and explored some of the major caves of Niue (which are many in number, some nearly two miles long), Brother Tongiatama and I were asked to accompany him. Brother Tongiatama, of course, had the greater knowledge of their locations and sizes.

There is a fresh-water system in place in Niue today. However, much of the water is still supplied by iron-roof rain runoffs into collection cisterns. Apparently there was not adequate fresh water available from the caves.

Stairway down a cliff.

Ten
HELP FROM TWO NEW ELDERS

ELDER SLADE AND ELDER BAILEY soon became
accustomed to Niue Island and its unique atmosphere and lifestyle. It was
certainly different from the American lifestyle in which they had both
grown up.

These two elders were young men who had great faith in God and
firm testimonies of the gospel. They came to Niue at their own expense to
give two years of their lives to help teach and strengthen others. As they
did so, they grew to love the wonderfully simple Niuean people. And as
our dear friends of Niue recognized the elders' selfless objectives, they
came to trust and accept Elder Slade and Elder Bailey as they trusted and
accepted Elder Christensen and me. In the process, the doors of learning
and communication began to open wider.

We also took the two new elders around the island to meet other
papalagi (European people). Most seemed happy that they had come. Of
course, Commissioner and Mrs. Larsen invited us all to visit them in their
home. The Larsens were pleased with these new American "boys" who had
such youthful energy and enthusiasm, and they welcomed them whole-
heartedly. We might never have achieved success in Niue without help
from Commissioner Larsen. He was, indeed, a good friend to the Church.

With new emphasis, we continued holding the usual MIA meetings
and activities that our young Niuean friends liked so much—activities
such as volleyball, baseball, football (American style), boxing (Niuean
style), square dancing, and singing songs both sacred and popular. Along
with enjoying these activities, we shared gospel principles and studied

Elders Goodman, Christensen, Bailey, and Slade.

scriptures. We gave many Niueans opportunities to accept leadership roles and to help us teach in other villages. We taught them to stand in front of groups of people and express their own ideas, thoughts, and testimonies. At first, all of this was quite new and strange to our Niuean converts. But most of them also found it refreshing; they loved these moments of self-expression and did extremely well.

Recognizing the Hand of the Lord

It is impossible to remember these events without acknowledging the hand of the Lord in inspiring these young Niuean men and women to help us in our struggles to accomplish His work. The Niueans who helped us in our missionary work loved and appreciated opportunities to do so, and we loved and appreciated them for their efforts. We admired the courage and faith they demonstrated as they helped us preach the restored gospel to their own people—for in so doing, they were subjecting themselves to the persecutions, cursings, and stonings that we had endured since our arrival more than a year earlier. These Niuean companions of ours possessed the same wonderful spirit that Wilson "Moumou" McMoore had demonstrated when he served as my second companion after Elder Barrett had to leave Niue for medical reasons.

We shall always remember and love these Niuean companions—both in this life and in the next, where many of them have now gone.

Missionaries on Both Sides of the Island

Elder Slade and Elder Bailey quickly caught on to our methods of missionary work. They joined right in and were soon teaching lessons, conducting meetings, helping with the activities, and taking on leadership responsibilities.

Moumou and Elder Christensen, August 1952.

On 1 July 1953 we divided into two companionships. Elder Christensen and Elder Bailey stayed in Alofi and worked on the western side of the island. Elder Slade and I moved to Lakepa and worked the eastern side of the island. We decided that after 30 days we would change places with each other.

With the two companionships working, we were able to increase dramatically the total number of teaching sessions we could hold. Later, as the new elders became more accustomed to the work, we would occasionally divide into four teaching groups, with each missionary taking some of our fine young Niuean members and friends as companions.

Elder Bailey, Togiatama, Moumou, and Elder Christensen.

Biking 100 Miles in 10 Days

In a letter Elder Slade wrote on 29 June 1953 to his future wife, Annette, he commented on our increased pace: "We have bicycles and I have ridden over 100 miles since I have been here." He had arrived just 10 days earlier.

Two months later, on 28 August 1953, he wrote: "We have such a schedule now, we are on the go from morn until night. We have an average of 16 meetings a week among the four of us. We have meetings in six villages, and we have to bike from village to village, and most of those meetings are held at night. We don't usually get home until quite late. . . . It's a great feeling to know you are doing the work of God for the good of His people."

Alofi congregation, 1953.

460 Meetings in about One Year

On 17 July 1953, Elder Christensen wrote: "I put all our minutes in one minute book. We have held 460 meetings here on Niue" (ECJ, 482).

To have held 460 organized meetings in just over one year's time was certainly another small miracle for us, considering the difficulties. We knew that the Lord wanted this work to go forward, so we gave all we had. In turn, He blessed us far beyond our humble efforts—and far beyond our mortal understanding. For this we were deeply grateful.

Elder Harold Bailey

Elder Bailey and Elder Slade did indeed bring new life into our efforts on Niue—not only through the doubling of efforts, but also with fresh ideas they brought with them and shared freely.

Elder Bailey had great energy. In fact, it was sometimes hard for us to keep up with him. He had profound love for the children and youth on the island and spent much time teaching them. He loved the gospel and taught it in his own special way. For example, he was somewhat of an amateur magician and loved to entertain the people, young and old. Afterwards, he would usually show them how the tricks worked, much to their amusement. He had some success organizing a Boy Scout troop, which the young boys loved. He also baked cookies for the children and youth and enjoyed watching their eyes light up when they received his homemade treats.

As district president on the island, I gave many assignments to Elder Bailey, and he accepted all of them cheerfully and focused his great energy toward accomplishing them. All the Niuean members loved him for his selfless efforts in their behalf.

Unfortunately, Elder Bailey did not escape some of the difficulties that *papalagi* (Europeans) usually endure when trying to adjust to living in "paradise." His trial was in a form not unlike that endured by Elder Barrett, my first companion in Niue, who had to leave the island because of it. On or about 1 August 1953, Elder Bailey encountered some of the poisonous coral rock of Niue Island and became seriously infected. His cut led to blood poisoning, which caused him to be dizzy and to faint frequently. Being very sick, he was confined to bed for a week to 10 days. We gave him several priesthood blessings, and the doctor treated him with penicillin.

On 13 August 1953, Elder Christensen recorded: "Elder Bailey is getting much better in Alofi" (ECJ, 496). He soon completely recovered and returned to work as usual.

A fiafia for Elder Bailey, shown doused with powder.

Elder Thomas Slade

Elder Slade was also an excellent missionary. He loved the Lord and the Church deeply and was valiant in bearing his testimony at every opportunity. He was a good teacher and had a kind, pleasant manner in his delivery. He also accepted every assignment and gave all his strength to carrying them out. He had sincere love for the people and wanted so much to see them progress.

Like most young missionaries, Elder Slade quickly observed the stark differences between what he knew of the outside world and what was known and experienced by those whom he was called to teach. He had a deep concern and desire to help the Niuean people know the gospel. This was often the subject of his journal entries and his letters home.

Elder Slade was also tried and tested, as all of us were. Only 34 days after his arrival on Niue, Elder Slade developed one of those "wonderful" boils that had plagued me so terribly. In his journal he made the following comments:

27 July 1953: "I think I have developed a boil or something of that nature, because it has been there for 3 days now and hurts very much whenever I sit down."

31 July 1953: "It was really hard to sit on my bicycle seat with this boil. I don't know why I got a boil. I guess it's just the tropics. It's the first one I've ever had and I hope the last, although Elder Goodman had 30 or 40 of them before he finally stopped. Real torture. Job never had anything on him."

2 August 1953: "I went to Avetele today and my boil hurt so bad I could hardly give them a lesson. When I got back to Alofi I sat down for a while, and when I tried to get up I just about couldn't make it."

3 August 1953: "I went down to the Fale Gagao (clinic) to see the doctor about my *faka foha* (boil). He was not there, but the nurse gave me some dressing for it."

I could really relate to the debilitating pain boils can cause, and my heart went out to Elder Slade. Even with his ailment, he went forward, determined to accomplish his work. Fortunately he had only had one other boil during his time on Niue.

Elder Slade became district secretary after Elder Christensen completed his mission. He then became district president when I completed my mission.

Everybody Pays a Little

While we are on the subject of fleshly infirmities, it seems that each of us elders had to pay a little something for being on Niue. Elder Christensen, who was hit a couple of times with stones, was later afflicted with a painful facial cyst. The cyst lasted many weeks and ultimately had to be surgically removed, a painful procedure that required six stitches. The incision afterward became infected and required more medical attention and the taking of penicillin. He probably still wears that scar today.

A Test for Toi

Despite adversity, our missionary work continued to progress on both sides of the island simultaneously. As we had planned, after 30 days Elder Christensen and Elder Bailey took our place in Lakepa, and Elder Slade and I took their place in Alofi. That evening, 1 August 1953, Elder Christensen recorded: "Today we got settled down in Lakepa. It is going to be rough. They are not used to having white men living in their village. We can't seem to get too close to the people" (ECJ, 490).

But it was a different story in the neighboring village of Toi. The London Missionary Society claimed the village of Toi as their own—as, indeed, they claimed the whole island. No other religion was needed or wanted. In fact, every effort was made to keep everyone else out, especially the Mormons.

But in Toi, the LMS church had no pastor because the village was too poor to provide sustenance for one. When we arrived in the village and achieved some success, leaders and members of the other church became angry and did all they could to get us out. One Sunday, they planned to hold meetings with the people of Toi to persuade them not to listen to us.

But Elder Christensen and Elder Bailey had other ideas. On the evening before the Sunday meetings in Toi were to take place, the elders went to Toi, accompanied by four of our wonderful brethren from Alofi—Solomona, Tuimaitoga, John Tanua, and Moumou.

"This evening a few of us went up to the village of Toi for a meeting and an evening of entertainment," Elder Christensen wrote in his journal. "There was a method in our madness. The purpose of the entertainment was [not only because we loved them] but also to keep the people up late that night. [We hope they forgave us.] Tomorrow some pastors of the other church are coming to the village to hold meetings with the people to tell them to pull away from the Mormons. They are going to hold meetings at 6 A.M., 9 A.M., and 2 P.M. Our intention was to stay with our people late enough so that they would not want to get up at 10 A.M., let alone 6 A.M." (ECJ, 490).

During the meeting, Elder Christensen admonished the people to be strong when the pastors came the next day. The people responded that they would remain faithful to the Church and to the teachings they had received. They all enjoyed a party late into the evening, and then the missionary group returned to their homes.

The next afternoon, after the meetings and attempts to remove the Mormons were over, Elder Christensen, Poitolu, Sionevia, and Sione returned to Toi for a meeting. "We found the people still as faithful as can be," wrote Elder Christensen. "The meetings were held by the other church's pastors. None of our people budged as far as I know" (ECJ, 492).

Indeed, the pastors' efforts had little or no affect on the dear Saints of Toi. They exercised their new faith in God and again demonstrated the wonderful Niuean quality of courage. It is little wonder that Toi became known as the "Mormon village."

A Surprise Stop at Mutalau

Elder Slade and I returned to our residence at Togiatama's in Lakepa and resumed teaching in the villages of Lakepa, Toi, and Liku. Since we were having such great success in Toi, we spent much time there. Each time we went to and from Toi, however, we had to pass through the village of Mutalau. Since the people in Mutalau were not very friendly to us, we were always relieved when we got to the other side of the village.

As we were passing through Mutalau late one evening after holding meetings in Toi, several villagers stopped us and requested that we visit a young woman who was seriously ill. At first, their request surprised us and made us somewhat suspicious. But the villagers seemed sincere, and they appeared to be truly concerned about the sick woman.

We consented and went with them to a small hut that contained very little except the usual woven mats and a kerosene lamp. In the center of the room was a young woman lying motionless upon a mat, with her head resting on a small pillow. Her name was Finioni, and she was approximately 20 years old. Her parents told us that she had been unconscious for several weeks. They desired that we give her a blessing and make her well.

I paused and considered the situation. Here we were in Mutalau, one of the villages that had long resisted any attempts—from our missionaries and our members—to be friendly or to teach them. To the best of my memory, the village of Mutalau was one of the places where we had earlier been stoned and cursed. We had good reason for wanting to pass through quickly and for being suspicious when they asked us to stop that night.

As we sat with the family on the floor of that small hut in the dim light of the lantern, the thought came to me that we needed to know more about this family. How did they feel about God and Jesus Christ? How did they feel about us? Why did they send their neighbors to stop us and ask us to give their daughter a blessing? Why did they think we could heal her?

We talked for a long time—late into the night. They told us that they believed in Jesus Christ and felt that He could heal their daughter if they had enough faith. I distinctly remember asking them if they did have enough faith. When they answered that they did, I realized that we were witnessing another great example of that wonderful, simple, pure Polynesian faith. This father and mother knew nothing about the priesthood of God or of our callings. They did, however, feel that we were humble servants of God who were willing to give and endure much in His name.

I felt that even though many villagers in Mutalau had made great efforts to keep us away, the Spirit had prompted at least a handful of humble people to stop us and ask us for a blessing. We replied that we were more than willing to help and share what we had.

Kneeling on the mat with the family, we gave a humble prayer of thanksgiving. We prayed mightily that the Spirit might be present and that the will of the Lord might be done. We then anointed Finioni's head and blessed this daughter of God that she would be made whole. Within minutes she became conscious and sat up for the first time in nearly a month. We rejoiced with the family at her recovery and then continued on our way home to Lakepa.

We had great hopes that this miracle would give us opportunities to start teaching in Mutalau, but it was not to be. Finioni's family refused to allow us to teach them the gospel because they were afraid of the pastor and the other villagers.

Finioni's Coma Returns

A few days later, we learned that Finioni had gone back into a coma. Her family desired that we return and give her another blessing. This we did to show our love for them. Of course, we also hoped they would begin to listen to our message. After we administered again to Finioni, I felt impressed to tell the family that they needed to demonstrate greater faith in the Lord than before—and that they needed to fast and pray earnestly for 24 hours. We explained that a true fast would require complete abstinence from both food and water. We also told them that we elders would join them in the fast. They consented to do so, and we all began our fast.

Elder Slade recorded this series of events in his journal as follows: "21 July 1953 – On our way home [from Toi] we stopped in Mutalau and administered to this sick woman and prayed that she might be spared."

"23 July 1953 – Last night we went to Mutalau to see Finioni. She was still very ill, so we administered to her again. We started a fast and prayer day for a 24-hour period."

"24 July 1953 – This morning we started the day with a fast and prayer for Finioni in Mutalau. It has been a real testimony to me this week because we administered to her every night and fasted for 24 hours and now she is becoming strong and she said her first words in over a month. There is not a person or thing in this world that can tell me this is not the Lord's work because [if he did] he would be a liar. Amen."

"25 July 1953 – This morning we continued our prayer for Finioni. I

Elder Slade at a Niuean hut.

Shoreline looking north in Alofi.

know that through the faith of her parents and us she will be well again. We went to see her again this afternoon and administered to her again. She is getting along fine now."

"28 July 1953 – We had a good crowd at Toi and received a couple more names for baptism. We also administered to Finioni in Mutalau."

Unfortunately, after all of our efforts to help Finioni get permanently well, to get her family to give us an opportunity to teach them, and to find others in the village of Mutalau to teach, we were not successful. Finioni's family was sincerely appreciative of our efforts and thankful to the Lord for blessing Finioni. However, they and the other villagers were not receptive to the gospel message. The hold of the other church was too strong to give us entrance yet.

We expressed our love to Finioni and her family, but we saw them very rarely after that last meeting. I don't believe Finioni or any of her family joined the Church, at least while Elder Slade and I were there.

This experience led me to believe that the Lord was waiting for Finioni and her family to respond to the source of their blessings before He would give a complete and permanent healing to her. I felt that in order for the sealing of the blessing to be complete, they needed to recognize the Savior's work, listen to our message, and acknowledge the priesthood of God from whence the blessings came.

I liken this situation to the many times people in the world today—and even some members of the Church—enjoy great blessings from God but fail to acknowledge His hand in all things. Yet these things are so obvious.

Brother Hukui of Mutalau

Some people in the village of Mutalau did eventually receive the gospel. Brother Hukui of Mutalau learned of the Church in Samoa and was baptized while visiting there. After his baptism, he returned to Niue in June 1953 on the *Tofua* that bought Elder Slade and Elder Bailey. Hukui was a very strong man who later helped the elders get started in his home village. He was one of the first on the island to receive the priesthood.

Baptizing 18 People at Mukefu Cave

At about this time, we began preparing for another baptism. This one would be on the north end of the island in the cave at Mukefu. Because of his illness, Elder Bailey could not take part.

Elder Goodman in the mouth of one of the many caves in Niue.

On 11 August 1953, Elder Christensen recorded: "On arriving at Mukefu, we met Elders Slade and Goodman. We interviewed the people, had a meeting, then went down into the Mukefu cave and baptized 18 people. Seven men were from Toi. After the baptism we went up to a home in Mukefu and confirmed them members of this wonderful church. We now have about 124 people baptized into the church here on Niue" (ECJ, 496).

Eleven
MURDER IN PARADISE

AT AROUND 2:30 A.M. on Sunday morning, 16 August 1953, someone from the administration came to our quarters in Alofi and awakened Elder Bailey and me with the horrifying news that a group of young men had attacked and murdered Commissioner Larsen. Mrs. Larsen had also been wounded and was in critical condition. Their daughter Thelma was all right, as was their young son, Billy, who had run down the hill to Alofi to sound the alarm.

Our messenger said he thought the murderers planned to kill all of the *papalagi* (Europeans) and that we should come with him to gather together for protection. We quickly pulled our clothes on and went to a house with a wide vista around its perimeter. The women and children were gathered inside. We younger men stood guard outside. Because I'd had military training, Police Chief Harry Williams gave me a .45 caliber military pistol, which I kept in my belt while on guard duty.

When it became light, we went up to the Larsen home, where we found a terrible scene. Mr. Larsen's body had by then been placed in a body bag, which was in a wooden box in the hall. The bedroom was a horrible scene with blood everywhere.

Mr. Archie Jacobson, who worked for the administration, was the only person at the Larsens' home when we arrived. He explained that at about 1:00 A.M. that morning, six prisoners had broken out of the prison farm. Three of them, armed with big bush knives, headed for Mr. Larsen's home, which was only a short distance away. After cutting the telephone line, they entered the home and went directly into the bedroom, where

Grave site of Commissioner Larsen

Commissioner and Mrs. Larsen were asleep. They surrounded the bed and started hacking away at Mr. Larsen. He was nearly decapitated and lived only one hour after the attack. He was able to tell the doctor who his attackers were.

Mrs. Larsen had jumped out of bed and began defending herself by raising her arms against the bush knives. She also began yelling and screaming loudly. Her screams probably saved her life and the lives of her children, because the attackers were scared away. However, she had received many life-threatening wounds. Her arms were broken in four places, and she had a wound on her forehead. She was hospitalized for a few weeks and eventually recovered physically. However, I don't know if she was ever able to get rid of the nightmare of the experience. Our hearts went out to her and her family.

Elder Christensen and Elder Slade were taking their turn staying in Lakepa and working on the other side of the island. They got word of the murder about an hour after Elder Bailey and I did. Elder Christensen recorded the following in his journal: "Brother Togiatama came knocking at our door about 3:30 A.M. and told us the very sad news that Mr. Larsen had been killed. Mrs. Larsen was in critical condition in the hospital in Alofi. Mr. Williams, chief of police, sent Elder Slade and me a warning to make it to Alofi as soon as we could possibly get there. So we packed up a few things, got on our bicycles, and took off along with Togiatama and Poitolu" (ECJ, 499). They arrived safely in Alofi.

Elder Slade also recorded his version of the events: "About the . . . most horrible thing that I have ever seen or heard of was the sudden murder of our resident commissioner, the good Mr. Larsen. Because of Elder Bailey's infected foot, I was staying with Elder Christensen in Lakepa. On Sunday, 16 August, at 1 A.M., Mr. C. H. Larsen was attacked while in bed asleep and brutally chopped to death with a big native bush knife by some of the native boys who were in prison and broke out. Mr. Larsen's wife was also seriously injured by the same boys. She is in the Niue hospital now with severe lacerations."

The three attackers' names were Folitolu from Hikutavake, Tamaeli from Liku, and Latoatama (known as Suka) from Tuapa. Suka was reportedly the one who had killed Mr. Larsen. Suka had previously inscribed the following in Niuean on his bush knife:

"I AM SUKA THE NIUEAN HERO, GREATEST LOVE TO THE PEOPLE OF NIUE. GOOD LUCK. I AM GOING TO DIE FOR MY PEOPLE."

As resident commissioner, Mr. Larsen was the judge of the high court of Niue. As judge, he administered the law and gave prisoners their sentences. He was a strict disciplinarian. Some say he was a bit rough on them. Some say he was too rough. These prisoners, all under age 25, were men with fairly long prison terms to serve. They had apparently decided to escape and get rid of Commissioner Larsen to pay him back for his alleged cruelty to them. Surely their actions were premeditated.

As dawn began to break, we all gathered at the police station, where groups of Niuean men were being organized into search parties. They searched all day but had no success finding the killers.

Search parties being organized by Brother Solomona to hunt for murderers.

Funeral and Burial

Island law required that the dead be buried on the same day death occurred because there were no embalming facilities or funeral homes. Mr. Larsen's funeral was held at 3:00 P.M. Nearly all the people of Niue—people from every village on the island—were present. Many formed a funeral procession that accompanied the body from the hospital at the south end of Alofi to a church building near the administration office. Most of the islanders walked slowly and reverently behind the caravan of vehicles. We rode in one of the government cars.

Mr. Larsen was laid to rest in a royal spot of ground in the center of Alofi—ground reserved for those of high status. His grave was dug in the very hard, solid rock next to the grave of King Tuitoga, who had reigned from 1876 to 1887. This was a fitting place for our friend, who had nobly served the people.

Digging Mr. Larsen's grave.

On the evening of the funeral, Elder Christensen wrote: "Mr. Larsen was a wonderful man and our very good friend. He did a great deal in making it possible for the Latter-day Saints to get started here on Niue. He was a happy man at all times and will be greatly missed by all who knew him" (ECJ, 506).

Members of the court at Mr. Larsen's grave site.

The First Day under Siege

Although Niue is a small island, there were plenty of places for the murderers to hide. Elder Christensen recorded: "There are so many caves on the island as well as thick bush and plenty of *kai* (food) that these killers could stay in the bush for a long time and never be found. 100 square miles of rock and bush is a lot of territory to cover. It's not going to be easy to find them. But they will probably want some cooked food and a smoke, so they'll more than likely give themselves up. I hope they are caught soon. It sure makes a guy nervous when he knows he is wanted by some killers" (ECJ, 507).

The day after the murder, 17 August 1953, Elder Christensen recorded: "This morning a search party from each village went out looking for the three murderers of Mr. Larsen (Suka, Folitolu, and Tamaeli). Search parties were out all day and found no signs of them at all. I went over to the 'batch' [bachelors' quarters for the European government workers] as soon as it got dark. Again, I was up for most of the night keeping watch. They are really after all the *papalagi*. Mrs. Larsen's condition is improving a little today" (ECJ, 507).

All-Night Guard Duty

All of us elders stayed up all night on guard duty and tried to get some rest during the day. My guard duty was at the house where the women and children were staying. I still had the .45 caliber pistol in my belt. We tried to comfort and reassure our Niuean members and even some of our *palagi* friends that things were all right. We felt that the murder was the work of a few enraged escaped prisoners who would soon be caught. And we assured one another that we needed to have faith that the Lord was with us and would take care of us.

Many Niueans later told us that the other *papalagi* on the island were not really in great danger because the killers were focused primarily on the resident commissioner. However, since the commissioner's wife had also been attacked, it was a good assumption that others might also be harmed. The precautions taken were proper under the circumstances.

The Second Day under Siege

This was quite an experience for men as young as we were. Elder Christensen recorded a poignant moment in his journal the following day, 18 August 1953: "My birthday today. I am 22 years old. . . . The search

Some of the papalagi (Europeans) living and working in Niue.

continues again today for Tamaeli, Suka, and Folitolu. Someone thought they saw them at Liku, so trucks took all the Alofi men up to Liku to search for them. Some had guns, some clubs, many had bush knives, so they were ready to hunt. At the end of the day there was no sign of them. So tonight I went over to the 'batch' to keep watch again" (ECJ, 509).

The Third Day under Siege

Elder Bailey recorded the following in his journal: "We had to take turns at guarding the [*palagi*] ladies of the village. [This we did] all night. The three men who got out said that they were going to kill all the white men on the island. We had pistols and rifles to guard with. Whenever the church bell would ring it would mean that the three men had been sighted. There were many wild goose hunts" (pages 49–50).

Elder Christensen wrote on 19 August 1953: "No sign of the murderers yet. A woman from Hakupu was in the bush getting food and said she saw Suka. He asked her if she had any cigarettes. He frightened her so she ran back to the village. All the people were brought over to the Hakupu area. They looked all day for them but couldn't find them. Mrs. Larsen has been improving quite a bit" (ECJ, 509).

The Fourth Day under Siege

The following day, 20 August 1953, Elder Christensen recorded: "I had been up most all of the night on guard duty. I had just gone to bed when Mr. Empin got me out of bed [at 6:00 A.M.]. He said the three murderers of Mr. Larsen have been caught and are now in the village of Fatiau. I went over to the administration with Mr. Empin to do some work with Mr. Williams [chief of police]. Others took trucks and went out to pick up the prisoners" (ECJ, 510).

How the Murderers Were Captured

Elder Christensen later recorded the details concerning the capture of the murderers: "The constable at Fatiau was having one last look around his village before getting some sleep [at approximately 5:00 A.M.,] when one of the prisoners, Suka [the leader], came out of the bush. He yelled at the constable, calling him by name, saying, 'Don't shoot and don't be afraid. We want to have a talk with you.' As soon as he said this, Folitolu and Tamaeli came out of the bush. They all then went up to the constable's home for a talk. They had no bush knives on them. In fact, all they

Murderers of Commissioner Larsen getting ready for trial.

123

had in their hands was a Bible that Folitolu was holding. He was the pastor of the group, of all things.

"The weather here on Niue has been very cold the last couple of weeks, really too cold to be a tropical island. Apparently these men had been so cold and chased around so much these past four days that they couldn't take it any longer. Also one of the main reasons for the surrender was for a smoke. They said they couldn't go on any farther without having a cigarette. This was the first thing they asked for when they got into the constable's home. Also they couldn't take it any longer because [some] Niueans are very superstitious and believed they could not stay in the bush at night without being afraid of the *Aitu*, the spirits of the dead.

"The constable had a talk with them for a while, then put handcuffs on the two bigger men and called up Alofi with good news of the capture. Folitolu was pastor, so he read the Bible for them while they were waiting for the police to come from Alofi. [In Alofi] they were taken to the little jail house in the back of our home. They had about 10 guards watching over them. People came from all over to have a look at these sad men. The killers of Niue" (ECJ, 513–14).

It felt good to get back home in our own beds and get a good night's sleep. However, before going to bed that evening, Elder Christensen, Elder Slade, and I biked out to Avatele for a meeting. It was the first meeting we'd had for almost a week.

Displaying the Prisoners

The prisoners, all under 25 years of age, were a sad-looking group. However, they acted very proud and arrogant and called themselves "Niuean warriors." They had convinced themselves that their own people would be sympathetic and have mercy on them. They would soon find out differently.

As the authorities were bringing the prisoners to Alofi, Chief Williams decided to stop at the village of Avatele so the villagers could see the prisoners in captivity. The villagers all gave loud, threatening yells of displeasure, giving the murderers quite a scare.

The truck with the prisoners arrived in Alofi at about 7:00 A.M. Mr. Slaven, acting resident commissioner, had all the people of Alofi gather at the administration building, where they could see the murderers. Again, his objective was to make examples of them before the rest of the people.

Captured killers arrive in Alofi.

As soon as Folitolu, Suka, and Tamaeli were taken out of the truck for exhibition, all the people began to sneer and yell at them. Then Joe Jackson really let them have it verbally. Some of us felt that the people wanted to hang them right on the spot, but of course they didn't.

It later became clear that putting the prisoners on display for public ridicule and verbal abuse was a mistake—because the families of the prisoners had to listen to this and bear the shame of it in their small communities.

Reactions of the Niuean People

When the news of the resident commissioner's murder was first made known, the initial reaction of many Niuean people was to find and lynch whoever had committed the crime. Murder is contrary to the Niueans' nature, no matter what the circumstances. Many of the islanders wanted to bring swift retribution to the murderers because of the great shame the act had brought upon them.

Fortunately, the murderers were not found for four days. This period was long enough to give the Niueans time to evaluate the situation properly and to cool down. After the killers finally gave themselves up and explained their motivations, the attitudes of some of the people began to soften—at least enough to seek appropriate justice, rather than lynching them.

For the most part, the people of Niue were in a state of deep hurt and shock. There was an aura of great sadness among them. Most of them recognized that Commissioner Larsen had worked hard to ensure and strengthen their basic freedoms, such as freedom to live by the rule of law. He had also been a champion of freedom of religion, including freedom from fear of oppression by religious cursings. Many Niueans agreed that changes were needed.

However, in the eyes of some, Commissioner Larsen had ended up creating fear of a different kind. Some felt that he was trying to make dramatic cultural changes in a system that, of itself, wouldn't easily change.

Most agreed that Commissioner Larsen had been a strict disciplinarian, but they also knew that there was no justification for murder. Although many had not appreciated the methods he had used to accomplish his goals, I believe many islanders appreciated him more than they had shown. Therefore, they were angry, embarrassed, and ashamed of this terrible act.

Commissioner Larsen, Niue's Good Friend

It would be many months before things would really get back to normal. The Niuean people carried an aura of sadness and shame for a long time; even today, some have a hard time thinking about or discussing the matter.

The murder was indeed a great tragedy. I'd had the pleasure of spending many hours of discussion and recreation with Mr. Larsen. I enjoyed being in his company and learned many things. During these times I learned of his great desire to serve and strengthen the Niuean people. He knew the people, and he wanted to help them progress. In turn, most of the people respected him for the good things he tried to do for them.

He had one large obstacle, however, one in which we were involved—providing freedom of religion. The one religion, while having exclusive domain on the island of Niue for more than 90 years, had good intentions in trying to keep all other religions off the island. They believed that a choice of religions would create friction and discord among the villagers and destroy peace and harmony. It was as if the Niueans could not be trusted to govern or be governed by a rule of law, but that they had to be governed by fear of heavenly retribution. This erroneous thinking would certainly explain why the use of religious cursing was so prevalent. But as a result, the people lived in fear and oppression. The government was not able to function fully if it did not please the existing ecclesiastical hierarchy.

I believe that Mr. Larsen tried very hard to help the people break through that oppressive social order and live in greater freedom under the rule of law and truly have freedom of religion.

Commissioner Larsen, a Friend of the Church

We all greatly missed Commissioner Larsen. He had been a strong advocate for the Mormon Church's presence in Niue. He knew us and trusted that we would contribute in positive ways to the lives of the people. He was indeed, our good friend. I sincerely believe that the Church would not have been established in Niue without the help of Commissioner Cecil Hector Watson Larsen. I believe that the Lord had a hand in directing him to us—or us to him. We will always remember him.

When President Ottley learned of Mr. Larsen's untimely death, he wrote the following in a letter to me from Rotorua, dated August 21 1953:

"The terrific shock of the year is the Larsen tragedy. I can't quite realize that such a thing has happened, yet such things do happen in a crazy, mad world, and nothing can stay them until the promised Millennium when the devil will be bound. Any courtesy the mission can render the family, we shall be more than happy to do. They have certainly been friends to us."

A Prophetic Statement by President Ottley

When I received this letter from President Ottley, I remembered something he had written to me more than five months earlier, on 11 March 1953. When discussing our work on Niue, with its successes and difficulties, he made a rather prophetic statement:

"This matter of crude hoodlumism is a natural consequence of the type of tactics normally engaged in by the opposition. I never saw it fail. It always follows the same pattern. One would think that Satan, with all the help he has, could be a little more original. It will pass over, but *some-one may have to be stricken* before it does. I hope not. That is the Lord's problem, not ours."

A Trial for the Murderers

Since Niue had no airstrips or harbors, the closest police backup help was on the islands of Samoa, three days away by boat. A small motor vessel with additional police and detectives left Samoa the day after the murder and arrived in Niue on 21 August, one day after the killers were apprehended.

On 4 September, a second boat, the *Maui Pamare*, arrived at Niue bringing a judge, court clerks, and lawyers so that a trial could be conducted. The trial began on 7 September at the Tufukia school. We were

Maui Pamare arrives at Alofi.

able to attend many of the sessions and found them interesting and informative. The trial ended two days later. All the defendants were found guilty and were condemned to "hang by the neck until dead."

A New Trial

After the trial, there was much controversy concerning whether the hanging should take place in Niue, New Zealand, or Samoa. Still later, there came much public outcry against the use of capital punishment, and an appeal was made. As a result of the appeal, the sentence of death by hanging was revoked and was changed to life in prison. As of this writing, all three murderers are deceased.

Twelve
TRYING TO GET BACK TO NORMAL

WITHIN LESS THAN A WEEK of Mr. Larsen's death, we missionaries were back on a full schedule, working in all six villages where we had established the Church. We were even starting to work in several new areas. On 26 August 1953, Elder Christensen recorded: "This evening we held MIA here in the village of Lakepa. It was their first MIA here, they surely did enjoy it. A very interesting and delightful day" (ECJ, 518).

Later, on 28 August 1953, he recorded: "Poitolu, Elder Bailey, and I went over to Liku to spend the day. On arriving there we went down to the sea, which is about two miles from the village, with a few of our brethren. We had a good time. Back in the village we played a game of baseball and held a few boxing matches. They fixed us a very good Niuean *kai* [food], including moa, kumara, talo, and takihi. This evening we held an MIA which was very nice. But, as usual, we had some stones thrown at the house where we were having our meeting" (ECJ, 519).

Elder Slade and Elder Bailey soon became accustomed with the practice of being targets of stone throwing and of being the object of the usual cursings by the other church. Fortunately these incidents became less frequent than when we first arrived on Niue.

Time Out for a Chore That Had to Be Done
Since there were no sewer systems in Niue at the time, we had to rely upon the "little house" out behind the "big house" to accommodate Mother Nature. The time came when we needed to build a new privy. (We missionaries named it "George.") Digging a hole in the solid Niuean

rock was a task that took much effort and many hours of just plain sweat and hard labor. So difficult was the task that we thought we would try to find some dynamite to help it along.

On 15 September 1953, Elder Christensen reported: "Spent the day here at home. Went all over the country trying to find some dynamite so we can blast a hole for 'George,' our new outhouse" (ECJ, 529).

To my recollection we were not able to find the dynamite, so we had to go back to the old "armstrong" method of doing it by hand. On 18 September, Elder Christensen recorded: "I worked all day long digging a hole for our lavatory. The ground is solid rock. I didn't get very much done, but I did wear six blisters on my right hand. Tender little *palagi*" (ECJ, 530).

The project to build the new outhouse extended well beyond Elder Christensen's and my tenure as missionaries. Elder Slade inherited it. He wrote the following note in a letter to his parents some 10 months later, in July 1954: "We are digging a new outhouse. We have to blast about every two feet. Solid coral and it is hard. Last Tuesday I was using a 10-pound sledge hammer. Elder Harris was holding the drill we use to make dynamite holes. Elder Harris now has a broken hand. We realize it could have happened to any one of us, as it almost has several times, because we all take turns. It was unfortunate for Elder Harris. We want to go down about three more feet, and then it will be finished. It has taken about 10 months to dig 9 or 10 feet. Slow process."

The Work Continues with New Momentum

We began having wonderful success again. Among the four of us, using our new members as helpers, we would hold up to eight meetings a day on Sunday, reaching all the villages in which we had Church groups. It was a joyous time for us. Yes, it was tiring, exhausting, and difficult, but the people were so receptive and eager to hear more of the wonderful gospel of Jesus Christ. Being buoyed up by the Spirit and our love for the people, we gave all we had to these dear, loving, wonderful, faithful Polynesians. I know they loved us and deeply appreciated our humble efforts.

We held an even greater number of meetings during the week in the form of MIAs, which meant more contact with the people through sports and drama, storytelling and singing. We could feel the trust building and the lines of communication opening yet wider. We were so grateful to the Lord for His help and direction and, most of all, the opportunity to be able to serve.

A Niuean sunset.

Special Moments of Joy

At many points in our time on Niue, each of us missionaries would suddenly be struck by the raw and awesome beauty of the island of Niue itself. Because of its firm, naturally rugged, isolated setting, it has an indescribable beauty all its own.

In one of these moments of inspiration, Elder Slade, who was, in a

Shoreline looking North from Alofi.

133

way, speaking for all of us wrote: "I was sitting here reading . . . , when all of a sudden I looked up and out over the sea. I thought to myself, 'This is, I believe, the most beautiful day I've ever seen on Niue.' The ocean is of a most exquisite color of blue, and calm, and clear as a mirror. I looked up through the coconut palms out in front of our home at the beautiful clouds as they waft lazily over the island, drift out over the sea, and disappear beyond the horizon, and I thought, 'If the whole world were as peaceful and if the whole world had the gospel of Jesus Christ, what a wonderful world it would be. It wouldn't be a world, but a heaven.' I felt so thankful to our Heavenly Father for the many wonderful blessings He has given me, too many to enumerate" (in a letter to his parents, March 1954).

Elder Slade was enjoying a very special moment of peace and of joy unspeakable when he wrote those wonderful words. Those same moments came to each of us often. They came from the Spirit to comfort us in those very difficult places, during those very difficult times, so far from home.

Thirteen
NIUEAN FAREWELL SONG

THE "GREAT AND DREADFUL" DAY, which all missionaries eventually have to face, was approaching for Elder Christensen. It would be "great" because he would get to go home. But it would also be "dreadful" because he would have to leave the wonderful people he loved so much.

When we received word that Elder Christensen would leave on the *Tofua* on October 7, our dear members and friends extended many expressions of love to him. He faithfully recorded each one in his journal. Following are a few vignettes:

8 September 1953: "Most of the people of Lakepa and Toi thought I was leaving this ship (Sept. 9th) so they gave me basket after basket as a *fakalofa*. The Toi people had a *kai* prepared for me, which was very nice (yam, hard-boiled eggs, coconuts]. Some people would give me an egg, some a tomato or a nice basket" (ECJ, 525).

23 September 1953: "It is going to be hard to leave these wonderful, simple, loving people" (ECJ, 534).

27 September 1953: "This afternoon Wilson Moumou fixed a farewell *kai* for me here at the elders' home. It was his *fiafia* to me. He broke down in tears because I was going; he wanted me to stay here. . . . Brother Tupago broke out crying when bidding farewell to me" (ECJ, 535).

3 October 1953: "Today people came from all over the island to have a *fiafia* for me. There were about 300 that came here to dance. We had a few sports; then about 1:00 everyone had a beautiful Niuean *kai*. After the *kai* came the dancing, and boy oh boy was it great. Each village that we teach in, six in all, gave an item. The dancing started at 2 P.M. and ended up at 6. I really had a day of it, and it was wonderful. I received over 100 gifts of baskets, hats, etc. The people certainly gave

me a wonderful *fiafia*, one I will never forget" (ECJ, 539).

These thoughtful demonstrations of love and appreciation that were extended to Elder Christensen were also extended to me, as my own "great and dreadful" day was approaching in a couple of months.

In fact, all of us missionaries were so overwhelmed by these great acts of seemingly unfeigned love that we marveled at them continually. Probably nowhere in the world is there a people like the Polynesians. They are a beautiful people because of their simple, unrelenting love—love of life, love of each other and of all people of goodwill, love of nature and all things beautiful, love of God, who provides so abundantly. These things we have remembered all of our lives.

Elder Christensen Leaves

On 7 October 1953, Elder Christensen recorded in his journal: "The Big Day – I got into the lighter, waved good-bye with tears in my eyes, and out to the *Tofua* we went. As we left the wharf the Niueans sang their farewell song. It was beautiful. I had a beautiful lei around my neck, and oh it was hard to say good-bye to all my wonderful friends. I was on the rail watching until I could see Niue no more. It was sad saying good-bye to Elders Goodman, Slade, and Bailey, and old Moumou had to cry" (ECJ, 542).

Elder Christensen preparing to leave Niue.

A Three-man Team

After Elder Christensen's departure, Elder Slade, Elder Bailey, and I continued on as a three-man team. Maintaining our previous meeting schedule in the six villages would be difficult, so we began to include more of our young members as helpers. We gave the priesthood to the men and boys worthy to receive it. To the women we gave assignments in the MIA, Primary, and Sunday School. The people loved their callings and did well, for the most part, with their limited understanding. President Ottley and the elders in the mission office had been sending us pictures, books, and manuals (English only), which helped greatly.

Our hectic schedule would soon get even worse because my "great and dreadful day" was fast approaching and would occur the following month with the November ship.

Final Quarterly Report of 1953

As our meetings continued, more of our investigators were coming forth to be baptized. In the final quarterly report of 1953, we noted that we had approximately 200 members of the Church on Niue Island. What a wonderful blessing for the people! What a blessing for us missionary messengers!

Elders Christensen, Goodman, Bailey, and Slade, August 1952.

My Time to Leave Approaches

As was done for Elder Christensen, the people held many beautiful farewell *fiafias* and meetings for me. Each was filled with expressions of love and appreciation. My heart was deeply touched by each incident. At many of the meetings, my Niuean friends would render the most beautiful music on earth by singing the Niuean farewell song. Nothing would touch my heart more or bring a lump to my throat and tears to my eyes than that seemingly celestial music.

They gave me many, many wonderful gifts of *fakaalofa* (love) and, as always, gifts well beyond their own needs and wants. I treasure each one, and I still have them a half-century later. These gifts are beautiful things, all handmade, entwined with love and affection.

I hope that one day I might be able to return these things again to them to be enshrined in a case somewhere to remember that glorious period of so long ago.

My Own "Great and Dreadful" Day

Boat day for November 1953 came on the 17th. The ship arrived early and was tied at mooring off shore. It was the *Matua*, apparently replacing the *Tofua*, its sister ship. This would be my passage to Suva, Fiji, where I would board an airplane bound for New Zealand.

It was difficult to leave those faithful, loving people of Niue and those

Elders Goodman, Bailey, and Slade with Moumou.

loyal, selfless missionaries. "*Monuina e fenoga!*" they cried. ("Blessings on the voyage!") And yes, Moumou had to cry. I felt so sad to leave my loving, loyal friend and former companion. I will always remember him.

As I climbed aboard the lighter to go out to the ship, all the great memories of that wonderful rugged island began to play across my mind. I thought, "What a great adventure, what a great opportunity, what a wonderful blessing!"

As the ship pulled away, I too was at the rail watching, with a large lump in my throat and tears in my eyes, until I could see Niue Island no more. "*Mutolu kia* [Good-bye]! Until we meet again!"

Back to New Zealand via Suva, Fiji

After three days on the *Matua*, we arrived in Suva, Fiji, where I soon boarded the airboat to Auckland, New Zealand. I stayed at the mission home during Christmas.

One day while I was in the mission home, on 9 December 1953, the telephone rang and I, being the closest, answered. It was a call to advise us that Tumaki (President) Matthew Cowley of the Quorum of the Twelve Apostles had died.

For the next week I was privileged to watch the great Maori ritual of *tongi* (mourning) for Tumaki Matthew Cowley, who was so greatly loved and cherished by the Maori people. The love that the Maori people and all Polynesians demonstrated for this great Apostle of the Lord was beautiful and wonderful to behold.

In early January 1954, I boarded the *S.S. Oronosay* bound for San Francisco and returned home. Some weeks later I returned to Washington, D.C., and gave my mission report to President J. Willard Marriott and the Washington D. C. Stake high council.

Elder Matthew Cowley and his famous sign KIA NGAWARI—Be Humble.

Fourteen

AFTERTHOUGHTS

THERE WERE MANY great souls who labored diligently along-side us as full-time missionaries. They put at risk their own tranquility and personal safety to respond to the gospel message and must be remembered and memorialized in this book. We shall always remember the faithfulness and loyalty of these noble people as they struggled to respond to the message from the Savior concerning the Restoration of the gospel.

Some Later Significant Events on Niue:

■ July 1954: President Sidney J. Ottley of the New Zealand Mission and President Coombs of the Tongan Mission met on Niue Island to transfer Niue from the New Zealand Mission to the Tongan Mission.

■ October 1954: President Howard B. Stone, president of the Samoan Mission, passed through Niue on his way to the Fiji Islands, which would now be included in the Samoan Mission instead of the New Zealand Mission.

■ January 1955: President David O. McKay, the prophet of God to all the world and the President of The Church of Jesus Christ of Latter-day Saints, arrived at Niue Island. He was accompanied by Elder Franklin J. Murdock and President Coombs of the Tongan Mission. Because of rough weather they were not able to leave the ship and come ashore. Instead, they sent a loving, inspirational message to the Niuean Saints, which they received with joy.

■ 12 February 1955: "Work commenced on the Alofi Chapel with a handful of members raising money and doing much of the building by hand. They were assisted by labor missionaries. The building was com-

Elder Goodman and Fritz Krueger (at rear) attending a fiafia in Alofi.

President and Sister David O. McKay in Alofi Bay, unable to leave their ship.

pleted in 1958. Additional Church buildings were erected later" (*Deseret News 2001–2002 Church Almanac*, 375).

■ Etekati Piuti (Foli), sister of Ikimau, and one of the first 26 baptized in Niue (see chapter 4) married Feki Po'uha, former companion in Tonga of Elder John H. Groberg of the First Quorum of the Seventy. Feki is mentioned in Elder Groberg's books *In the Eye of the Storm* (later retitled *The Other Side of Heaven*) and *The Fire of Faith*. Feki and Etekati later moved to Salt Lake City, where she became an accomplished genealogist for the Niuean people.

■ 17 September 2002: When interviewed by *Meridian Magazine*, the reporter asked, "Did you ever see those who were throwing the stones at you?"

Robert Goodman answered:"We rarely ever saw those who were throwing stones at us. I guess we were too busy getting out of the way. Most stonings took place at night; however, there were some stonings during the day time [see page 80 when Elder Christensen got hit].

"When my wife and I visited Niue in December 2000, *fiafia* was held in our honor. At that time, while food was being served and each had an opportunity to speak, I met one of the stone-throwers for the first time. It was a sister who had later been converted to the Church. With obvious deep anguish, she stood up and while nervouly wringing her dish towel, bore her beautiful testimony and expressed sincere sorrow for having been one (as a girl) who threw rocks at us. She said that the pastor of the LMS church had told the young people to do this. She asked for forgiveness, which she promptly received with a big hug."

Prominent Members in Niuean Government

In an article published in the *Church News* on 18 September 1999, entitled "Church Grows Prominent on Coral Atoll of Pacific," Brother Douglas W. Banks listed several Niuean Latter-day Saints who have made great contributions in the Niuean government. At the time this article was written, Brother Lagavalu Haioti, the 42nd person baptized in the Amanau Cave, was serving as district president:

"From [its] simple beginning of persecution and difficulty, the Church has prospered, said Lagavalu Haioti, president of the Alofi Niue District of the Tonga Nuku'Alofa Mission.

"Pres. Haioti was eight years old in 1952 when he was baptized with his mother and sister. They were among the first Niueans to join the Church. Today, he serves as commissioner of Niue High Court and is the highest-ranking Niuean judge. He started serving as a part-time justice of the peace in 1975 while he was teaching school and is now the senior magistrate of the court. In his role as commissioner of the Niue High Court, he is responsible for 50 land commissioner judges and six justices of the peace. He also serves as the chairman of Forestry Projects, the chairman of Savings and Loan Society (the government credit union), and has been clerk of the Alofi South Village Council for the past 12 years.

"Pres. Haioti also directs the translation of LDS publications into Niuean. He explained in a *Church News* interview that he and his LDS colleagues involved in government service work for their country because of the principles they were taught by the Church.

" 'We have to contribute to the Church and the community at large,' he said. 'As members we have been encouraged by the prophet to work together with the government. We feel that is our responsibility.'

"More important, he said, the LDS influence in government is an indication that the people in Niue recognize and respect the Church.

"Veve Jacobsen, a member of the National Assembly, is another whose parents were early Church pioneers on the island. [Sister Jacobsen is daughter of "Rangi" Lagitafuke Viliko Fakahoa, OBE. See chapter 8.] Like Pres. Haioti's, her membership in the Church has taught her values and principles that have helped her in government service.

"Sister Jacobsen, a Relief Society teacher in the Alofi South Branch, studied nursing, eventually working in public health in New Zealand before returning to Niue in 1986. Not long after her return, she had a discussion with her father that led her to politics, she explained. He told her, 'If you stay in this country and you are unhappy with things then you must get into politics and help make better decisions for the country.'

"So, when a member of the National Assembly, the national legislative body, withdrew from office, Sister Jacobsen was elected to fill the vacant seat in a mid-term election.

"In every election since then, she has polled either the first or second largest number of votes of those elected. For the past six years, she has not only served as a member of the assembly, but also as the Minister of Health and Education, one of the premier's three cabinet ministers. In the past three years her role has also included being the deputy premier, a position that has brought her acclaim as the highest-ranking female government official in Niuean history.

"However, in the March 1999 election, even though she polled the highest number of votes of any of the elected National Assembly members, her party lost. She was nominated by her party to be the new premier but the party did not have enough votes to elect her.

"Other Church members, in addition to Sister Jacobsen, also have served in the nation's National Assembly: Liumaihetau Matagi served in the Assembly for 12 years, Fumaka Molai represented his village for nine years and Makamau Hekau served one three-year term.

"Another woman of prominence in the Niuean government is Maihetoe Hekau, who, until recently, served as the chairwoman of the Public Service Commission—which has responsibility for hiring , promotion, training and salary of all government workers.

"Also holding a number of prominent positions in Niuean government is Laga Lavini, president of the Niue South Branch. He is the general manager of the Niue International Airport, fire chief and a member of the Alofi South Town Council. He also serves as a member of the Civil Aviation Advisory Committee and is treasurer of the Niue Public Service Association.

"Like so many other Niuean government leaders, Pres. Lavini's mother also sacrificed for the Church as an early pioneer. Anamata Lavini, who today is the district Primary president, did much of the washing and mending for many of the early missionaries.

"Pres. Haioti noted the members in his country are examples of those following direction given in the Jan. 15, 1998, letter from the First Presidency, urging members of the Church 'to be full participants in political, governmental and community affairs.'

"One indication of this is the large number of young returned missionaries serving on the Niuean police force, said Pres. Haioti.

" 'They are the best quality,' he said. 'They respect the Word of

Wisdom, they don't drink and smoke. They are in good health. They have the opportunity to administer the law.

"'It is a very important assignment for each and every one of us to work in government. We are trying to help our members to live like Christ's example, to minimize criticism from others in the country,' he said. 'You have to show others the light [of the gospel] in order to raise the status of the Church among the people in Niue.'"

(At the time this article was written, Douglas W. Banks and his wife, Sandy, were members of the Oakton Ward, Oakton Virginia Stake. They had just returned in July [1999] from serving a mission in Niue. Brother Banks served as the official representative of the government of Niue to the U.S. government in Washington D.C. He is currently serving as president of the Tonga Nuku'alofa Mission.)

Religion in Niue Today

The following update is from the *CultureGram* on Niue, published by Brigham Young University in 2002: "Only a few vestiges of pre-Christian belief remain, such as a *tapu* (taboo) area in Hakupu that is still respected. Almost all Niueans belong to one of five denominations. The largest is Ekalesia Niue, the local offspring of the London Missionary Society that is most closely related to Congregationalism and counts 75 percent of the population as members. Ten percent [now 11 percent] belongs to The Church of Jesus Christ of Latter-day Saints. Smaller numbers belong to the Seventh-day Adventist Church, Roman Catholic, and Jehovah's Witness faiths. Due to its history and prominence in society, Ekalesia Niue has considerable influence in the political arena. Members of the main denominations mix freely in daily life, but they tend to socialize or work more closely with people of their own faith."

The current estimated population in Niue is 2000 people, and the population of The Church of Jesus Christ of Latter-day Saints in Niue is approximately 280. There are now four branches and one district of the Church on the island.

Many Niueans have migrated to New Zealand for better economic opportunities. Currently there are approximately 700 Niuean-speaking Latter-day Saints in New Zealand.

As of this writing, the following missionaries mentioned earlier in this book are deceased: President Sidney J. Ottley, Elder Harold Bailey, Elder Wallace L. Barrett, Elder Basil DeWitt, and Fritz Krueger.

Appendix

A. Entry Permit—Official Pass to Enter and Leave Niue

The Cook Islands Immigration Regulations 1939.

PERMIT TO ENTER NIUE ISLAND.

Form No. 3.

13 MAY 1952

NIUE

PERMISSION to enter Niue Island is hereby given subject to the above-entitled regulations

to ___Robert Maurice Goodman___ of Washington D.C., U.S.A. _____

NOTE.—No permit is of any force or effect in respect of a person who is a prohibited immigrant within the meaning of the regulations. As an authority to enter Niue Island this permit ceases to have effect on the expiration of two years from the day on which it was issued. If the Resident Commissioner is of opinion that a permit has been obtained by fraud or misrepresentation, it may be revoked.

Dated this___Thirteenth___ day of_____May_____, 19 52 .

_____
Resident Commissioner.

1 bk./8/39—8761]

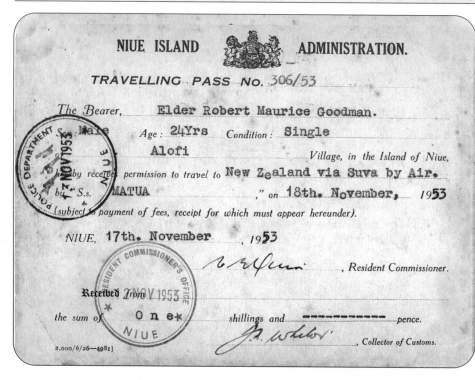

NIUE ISLAND   ADMINISTRATION.

TRAVELLING PASS No. 306/53

The Bearer, ___Elder Robert Maurice Goodman.___

Male ___ Age : 24Yrs ___ Condition : Single

___Alofi___ Village, in the Island of Niue,

hereby receives permission to travel to New Zealand via Suva by Air.

by "S.s. MATUA ," on 18th. November, 1953

(subject to payment of fees, receipt for which must appear hereunder).

NIUE, 17th. November, 1953

_____, Resident Commissioner.

Received from _____ 17 NOV 1953

the sum of One shillings and _____ pence.

_____, Collector of Customs.

2,000/6/26—4981]

150

B. First "Message to Israel"

A MESSAGE TO ISREAL   July 1952 Pg 1 of 2

HARKEN!! All the people of NIUE.....

As x servantsof the Almighty God we have come to tell you that God The
Father and His son Jesus Christ, has once again appeared and spoken to
His children on this earth. And through a PROPHET of God, Jesus Christ
has restored His Church on the earth again........
I beseech you, People of Niue, to listen unto our words and be not
afraid. This message is the most important event that has ever happened to the earth's people in these 'the last days'. It is most important to you and your children and above all to your ETERNAL SALVATION.

        We come not to cause disorder or displeasure among you
but to teach you the truth about the Gospel of Jesus Christ. The people
of NIUE have locked themselves in feeling secure that God will never
speak again. Do not be fooled to think that God will never speak again
to His Children, He has and does continue to speak through His Prophet today and guides His people and His church.

        Our Prophets and Apostles, with the guidance of the Lord,
leads the church with LOVE and UNDERSTANDING, not with fear or with
cursing. The Apostle Paul tells us to 'bless and curse not' (See
Roman 12:14) God never ment that His children should be ruled with
fear and with cursing. Jesus Christ gave His life to give us His
Gospel and He did it with LOVE not with the mighty power of God that
He had.

        Many false teachers have created their own gospel and have
called it the Gospel of Jesus Christ, to make for themselves money,
food and worldly goods, and if the people refuse they smite them with
worthless cursings and rule them with fear. Is this the way of Jesus
Christ? THINK! Think for yourselves!!! (read Matt. 7: 15-16)

        The Holy Bible, which is the ONLY Bible we have, tells us
that we must not sell the Gospel as Merchandise, or as a merchant
would sell a tin of meat. In PETER 2:3, we learn......'And through
covetousness shall they, with feigned words, make merchandise of you..
etc..'
        Are we followers of Jesus Christ or followers of MAN?
Jesus Christ told His Apostles to give the Gospel freely....do not
sell it....give it freely...We learn this in Matt.10:8...' freely ye
have received, freely give.' As more knowledge on the subject we
learn from 1st Peter 5:2, 'Feed the flock of God, which is among you,
taking the over sight thereof, not by constraint, but willingly; not
for filthylucre, but of a ready mind'.

-2- A message to Isreal.

       The Prophet Micah in the Old Testament tells us of days that will come when priests will teach for hire, and leaders will judge for money. This is bad in the sight of God. We learn this in Micah 3:11....More scripture on the subject read...1 Cor. 9: 18....

       This same trouble came up in the days of Christ when men who claimed to be the true followers of Moses, Sat in in the seat of Moses and placed heavy burdens upon the people and did not move one finger to help them. Christ was very displeased..Read Matt. 23: 1-4.

       The Lord wants His people to be humble, loving people, not a proud, boastful people who make themselves rulers over many. This also applys to His church leaders..(See Isaiah 24:2). Jesus Christ chose humble fisherman to be the leaders of His church...Peter, James and John..Paul the great Apostle worked with his own hands to support his household..(see 1 Cor. 4:11-12). Paul was a humble, loving man as was all the leaders of God's church. Do you think that is the way God wants His our leaders to be today?

       Do not think that by our words that we mean it is not right to give a gift; It is the teaching of Christ to do so. He tells us that when we give a gift to the church we must not do it so everyone will know. Do not sound a trumpet or make a loud noise so that men will see you and you will be praised of men. Give your gifts in secret and you Heavenly Father who sees in secret will reward thee. Read Matt. 6:1-4...'..Let not thy left hand know what thy right hand doeth'..

       Cease paying those whom you have hired and see how quickly he leaves because he thinks first of money, secondly of his people. 'The hireling fleeth, because he is a hireling, and careth not for the sheep'.....Read John 10:11-13...

       AWAKEN ALL YOU PEOPLE OF NIUE!!!!

Do not think that you are Heathen people, you are not. You are decendents of the 'TWELVE TRIBES OF ISREAL', God's choice people. The blood of Joseph, who was sold into Egypt by his brothers, flows thick through yourveins. You are choice in the eyes of God, do not forsake this heritage.

       'Come unto me all ye that are heavily laden...etc.' Matt.11: 28-30, also 1 Thess. 5;21....

       Let happiness abide in your hearts and be not afraid of any man, only God which is in Heaven......

                    A message from the Missionaries of;
                    THE CHURCH OF JESUS CHRIST
                      OF LATTER=DAY SAINTS....

C. Commissioner Larsen's Letter to Government Workers regarding Religious Beliefs

CIRCULAR MEMORANDUM

ALL DEPARTMENTS.

NATIVE STAFF : GENERAL

Owing to rumours now circulating among Niueans generally, several Administration employees have expressed concern that their services as members of the staff might be terminated because of their religious beliefs.

Please draw to the attention of all your staff immediately that employees of the Administration are free to belong to any religious denomination they choose. The conditions of employment for Niuean staff are the same as for European staff; employees can be engaged and discharged only in compliance with the Cook Islands Public Service Regulations.

KO E FAKAILOAAGA

KEHE TAU GAHUAAGA OTI.

TAU TAGATA GAHUA : KATOATOA

Tuga mo e tau tala go ne logona mai he tau tagata Niue, kua tokologa ni ia lautolu ne fai kotofaaga i loto he Fakatufono ne lahi e tupetupe he tau manatu he neke oti mai he tau gahua, he kua huhu atu a lautolu kehe falu a lotu kehe kehe.

Fakamolemole kia fakailoa vave kehe tau tagata gahua haau, ko lautolu ne gahua i loto he Fakatufono, kua ataina a lautolu oti ke oatu kehe ha lotu, kua fioia mo e tonu ke he ha lautolu a tau manatu. Ko e tau kotofaaga he tau tagata Niue kua tatai ni mo e tau papalagi. Ko lautolu e tau tagata gahua, kua omaoma kua mau e tau gahua, ka ko lautolu kua holia e tau Fakatufono he Atu Kula, ko lautolu ia ka uta kehe mai he tau gahuaaga.

(C.H.W. Larsen)
Resident Commissioner.
(Ko e Komitina)

D. Appointment as Marriage Officer

W A R R A N T

PURSUANT to Section 511 of the Cook Islands Act, 1915,

I, Cecil Hector Watson Larsen, Resident Commissioner

of the Island of Niue, do hereby appoint -

ELDER ROBERT MAURICE GOODMAN of ALOFI

to be a Marriage Officer for Niue, and to hold that

office from the twenty-second day of August, one

thousand nine hundred and fifty-two.

GIVE under my hand and the
Seal of the Cook Islands this
twenty-second day of August,
one thousand nine hundred and
fifty-two.

....
Resident Commissioner
of Niue.

E. Second "Message to Israel"

B̶A̶P̶T̶I̶S̶M̶ a Message To Israel - ‖ SECOND
MESSAGE
SEPT. 1952

Children to be Blessed:

Some will ask the question, "What, if anything, should be done for the children". The answer is that the Children should be blessed. Read Mark 10:13-16, Matt. 19:13-15:

In these scriptures of Jesus Christ, Himself, took the little children up into His arms & blessed them, He did not sprinkle them or baptize them... He Blessed Them.

It is quite apparent that the disciples of Jesus felt that the children were unworthy to go before the Master, so they rebuked them. To this Jesus was m"Much Displeased" and he ordered them to be brought to him for " Such was the Kingdom of Heaven". I am sure that He is equally displeased with the infant-baptisms and sprinklings of today. This information we learn from a Prophet of God, named Joseph Smith. The same man who, through heavenly guidance established the True Church and the True teachings of Jesus Christ.

Rebaptism:

Many people have spoken to me saying, that men have told them, if they are baptized again they will die. These foolish words are from men that know not the teachings of Christ or even the Bible, so in their ignorance they make up these false words to scare you. I would not have you ignorant of this subject.
Read Mark 1:4-8

This scripture, andmany others in the Bible, show us that if we were living in the time of John, the Baptist, and he Baptized us, then we would have surely heard of the Holy Ghost. If he said nothing about the Holy Ghost then we would know that he was not the real, John, the Baptist, but an imposter. Because one of the main reasons for the Mission of John was to tell of the gift of the Holy Ghost to be given by the one who followed who was Jesus Christ.
Read Acts 19:1-6

Here Paul asked if these baptized men had been taught about the Holy Ghost. They answered that they had not as much as heard that there be any Holy Ghost. Paul then, right away, knew that they were not baptized by John or any of the true servants of God, so he Baptized them again.

Bless & Curse Not:

I know that there would be some men, in the world, who are blinded by the craftiness of others that would attempt to keep you ignorant and afraid of turning your ears to the truth... These people will curse you and say that you will die by his cursing. But remember this, cursing is not taught in the Gospel of Jesus Christ. The Gospel of Jesus Christ is a Gospel of Love... What kind of a man is it that will curse his brother? The Apostle Paul (Romans 12:14) says to "Bless and Curse not"... Does this silly curser think that he is better than the Apostle Paul? Have these foolish men forgotten the words of Jesus Christ who tells us exactly what the first two and greatist commandments were? (Read Matt.22:36-40 & Luke 10:25-27)

How can these men, who have the nerve to call themselves the servants of God, curse and hate their brothers whom they can see and still claim that they Love God whom they cannot see?(Read 1 John 4:7-8,20-21) I say unto you, Brethren, turn away and cease this cursing and foolishness, if not, may God have mercy upon your souls at the final judgement.

F. List of Children Blessed in Makefu, October 1952

Childrens.

		age	Matua - Tane	Matua - Fafine
1	Sionisatini	6	Tohoraka	Gasisihetupe
2	~~Hatitu~~ Ikimata	5	Tohoraka	Gasisihetupe
3	Inagolotualoa	1.	Tohoraka	Gasisihetupe.
4	~~Fasiotinau~~	4	Panikitau	Aigatakai
5	Makatoni	4.	Panikitau	Aigatakai
6	Fenakitama	1	Pitasoni	Manatahemotu
7	Lene	5.		
8	Malamakeva	6	Konakava	Siolaheva
9	Fakaaiagatau	3	Konakava	Siolaheva
10	Mokasitalama	2.	Konakava	Siolaheva
11	Saurogahau	7	Fakalaga	Lauola
12	Tamani	5.	Fakalaga	Lauola
13	Falaunitama	4.	Kalauni	Ahitagaloa
14	Maosamole	3.	Vikita	Katagaloa
15	Kololino	2.	Vikita	Katagaloa
16	Manogiole	1.	Fakalaga	Lauola.

G. Plat for Alofi Chapel and Mission Home

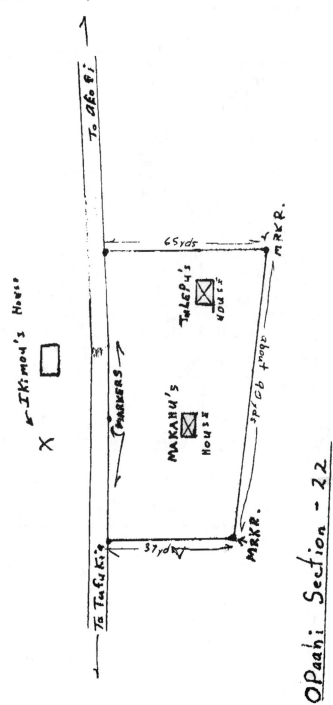

157

H. Correspondence for Land Acquisition for Alofi Chapel and Mission Home.

Dear Sister Adeline & Kou;

Fakaalofa Lahi atu kia mua. All is
well in Niue for the time being. Kauhiva and family are still
as faithful as ever as are all the other people in Liku, thanks
to your good work and the help of the Lord..

Adeline, on the other side of this
paper is a map of the section of land that we are going to try
and get for the church. The section of land where we built our
volley-ball court (the one next to Rangi's), is very hard to get,
infact it will be impossible to get a lease on the land that the
LMS won't be able to fight. The reason is that there is not legal
owner designated by the land-court, therefore, there is always a
possibility of our being chased off, if the land court did come to
Niue in the future. However, the piece of land across from your
old home has been through the Land-court and has established the
true owners and they have a 'Free-hold title' to it.

Now your legal mother, Folikimua, was
one of the owners, she has died now leaving you and your sister
Tefahega, as the only Heirs to her property, but, before you can
claim the property, you must sign an application for a Sucession
order. I have inclosed this application for you to sign and fill
out so please do, and HAVE A JUSTICE OF THE PEACE BE A WITNESS.
It is very necessary that you do this and have it on the next
Tofua if you agree fully.

Tefahega said that you and she divided
up Opaahi, you took the part next to Rangi's and she got the part
that we are trying to get now. That was an agreement between you
and her and the land-court does not reccognize that. When our
church signs a lease, then you can divide up the money according
to your agreement with Tefahega, but before we can talk about a
lease this inclosed appication must be signed by you. I hope you
will understand..We want to have the lease ready when Pres. Ottley
comes to Niue in June so we must act quickly. We are trying to
keep this as quite as possible in Niue.

We are well aware of your relatives in
Tamakoutoga and Lakepa, also of Ikimou, Foinela and Nikiniki. They,
with Tefahega, have all agreed to lease the land so I think with
the help of the Lord we will be able to provide something for our
good faithful people of Niue. May Our Father's blessings be with you.
Elder Goodman

P.S. Hope you are happy in New Zealand.

P.S.S. We have been keeping Kau's land clean.

158

Author with Rangi, in her home in Aukland New Zealand, November 2000.

Ikimautama Ikimau, New Zealand, 2000.

Makamau Hekau (Niue district president) and wife, Maihetai, 2000.

Author meets Fritz Krueger, for the first time in nearly 50 years, Aukland, New Zealand, November 2000.

Elder Thomas Slade, Elder Goodman, and Elder H. Thayne Christensen in the Salt Lake City area, 9 February 2002.

CHINA

JAPAN

TAIWAN

NORTH PACIF

NORTHERN
MARIANA
ISLANDS

PHILIPPINES   GUAM   M   I
                                        C
                                          R   MARSHALL
                                            O   ISLANDS
                                              N
CAROLINE ISLANDS   E   GILBERT
                                                  S   ISLANDS
                                                    I
                              M   E   L   A
NEW GUINEA   A   N   TUVALU
                                              E
                                                S
SOLOMON   I
ISLANDS   A

NEW HEBRIDES   FIJI
(VANUATU)   ISLANDS
                                                      TONG
NEW   ISLAN
CALEDONIA

AUSTRALIA

                          SOUTH   PACIF

International
Date Line

NEW
ZEALAN